She Lived Happily Ever After

A Memoir

Adda Christine Dahlke

Dedication

To Evan, the love of my life

and

to Jennifer, who told him to call me.

Contents

Part Four

Part One

In the Beginning

Matchmakers

A Marriage Bureau?

I always said that he had to be even more "into" Jesus than I was, gainfully employed, a non-drinker, smoker, or drug taker, and kind; that was penultimate. Handsome would be nice but not a deal-breaker.

In 2004, however, I wasn't really looking for love. I was thirty-nine years old, had a great job, a church, a ministry, family, friends, an apartment that I loved, a routine, and a cute little cat named Millie. I even had a garden, my first. I had just purchased a new Chevrolet S-10 pickup truck and joined 24 Hour Fitness. Life was great, not even a complaint. Well, I guess my job could have been a bit easier, and I had just visited with a surgeon who promised to help me with my "every day I have vertigo existence," so I guess all was not perfect. A better word would be content. I felt content with where I was in life or where God had me at the moment. This was a first for me, the contentment thing. I had never felt that way. There was always someone or something that I still needed to forgive, something about my body that I didn't like, or my worry about being perfect. Somehow, right now, I was feeling happy and a little more carefree.

He was divorced, with two daughters, and was not looking to get into another relationship. A routine haircut and after-church lunch with friends would change everything.

March 11, Thursday evening, he had a hair appointment with his longtime friend Jennifer. She mentioned that she thought he should get married again. He said that he wasn't interested in any relationships. He wanted to be like the Apostle Paul in the Bible, single and devoted to God and whatever He would have him do. He was also raising two daughters. He was busy but enjoying himself. She pressed, saying that he needed to remarry and that she had the perfect person for him.

"One of my other clients is 'weird like you.' You should call her."

"Weird like me?"

"You know, a Jesus person, an all-encompassing Jesus person. You will like her; she's great."

"No, thank you, I'm going to be like Paul."

March 14, Sunday. I woke up early, as usual, so that I could get ready to go to the worship team sound check before the Sunday Service started at 9:00 am. I warmed up my voice by doing some vocal exercises and singing some of the worship set that we would be doing that morning. I felt great, excited about church and seeing my friends and extended family.

He was there that morning for the second service with his daughter, Ashley, who I already knew from having her in my former Junior High Sunday School class. She was just a darling and came up to me for a quick hug and hello after the service was over. Interestingly enough, I had his other daughter, Brittnye, in one of my other youth groups, so I knew both of his beautiful girls before we had ever said two words to each other. I knew his name, though, Evan Dahlke.

I went to lunch with my bestie, Melanie, and her husband, Chuck. He went to lunch with his best friend, Gary, and his wife, Chris. Halfway through lunch, Chris told Evan that she believed he was too nice to be alone and that he should get married again. He repeated his speech about being Paul when she interjected, "There's this lady, her name is Adda, and you should call her." He responded, "That's sickening!" Nice, huh? She assured him, "I don't know her very well, but she's really nice. She sings on the worship team."

"No," he said, "that's not what I mean. Jennifer just told me the same thing on Thursday night. Did you speak to her?" She assured him, again, that she hadn't spoken to Jennifer and that she had just thought about this during church that morning. Believing that this could be a sign from God, he called Jennifer to ask for my phone number.

March 19, Friday. Went to work, as usual, had dinner with Mel and Chuck, then headed over to church for worship practice. I treasured this time with the rest of the team. We had been together for several years, and we clicked really well. I'm a falsetto soprano, if there is such a thing, and the only one who sang in that particular range, so I was on just about every Sunday. I don't usually gravitate toward the stage, so this took some getting used to at first. Now I couldn't imagine doing anything else. We all had a great time, but now I was a little tired from the week and was really looking forward to getting home, seeing my cat, and calling my mom to check in. I got into my truck and noticed the blinking light on the cell phone, indicating that I had voicemail messages. I figured it would be Mom, so I was completely surprised to hear a message from Evan Dahlke, whom I had only spoken to once or twice, telling me that he'd had a job go really well and wanted to go to PF Chang's to celebrate. Would I be interested in going? So, at this moment, I started panicking while noticing the time (it was around 9:00 pm) and was afraid that my conversation skills with men, being what they were, I would be stumbling about trying not to be defensive and goofy if I called him back.

I was almost always defensive when it came to men. I hadn't been interested in anyone for quite some time, and the last time I was, I made a complete fool of myself. I didn't trust myself at all to have a decent conversation with this man, but I took a chance and called him back. I'm so glad that I did.

Our Romance

Whirlwind /ˈwɚrəlˌwɪnd/

Something that involves many quickly changing events, feelings, etc.

March 19, at 9:00 pm I called the number, and he answered. We talked for two hours. I remember very little of what was said, except for his stating that he needed to hang out with more Christian singles, and at that time, I thought, "Well, if you want to hang out with me, just say so." I told him that my best friend's birthday party was the next day and asked him if he wanted to come. He said yes, and I shared the address and the time with him.

"See you tomorrow."

Phone call ended, and now I was sitting on my couch wondering what to do and what would become of this conversation. I had been desperately wanting, for years, to get married, but I felt defensive, and pretty much planned on just being friends with this guy. Not because of anything he said or who he was. I was just nervous and scared about relationships with men. More about that later.

March 20, Saturday – Day of Gina's party.

My two best friends, Melanie and Gina, had both gotten married in the last few years, so I was the only single person in our group that now included Chuck, Mel's husband, and Mike, Gina's husband. I called Gina's Mom, Tina, to let her know that I had invited someone to the party, but I didn't warn Mel or Gina that I was bringing someone. I had decided to just be myself, so my attire was a bit understated-tank top, cut-off jean shorts, very little makeup, and hair in a high ponytail. I drove to Tina's, arriving a bit early. Evan was already there. He got out of his truck and walked over to open my car door. He looked amazing in his button-down shirt and jeans. I got out of the car looking like Scout from To Kill a Mockingbird, and here was this gorgeous man escorting me to the house. I saw Tina looking out the window with an expression of shock and awe.

We walked into the house, and I introduced Evan to everyone. Mel wanted to play a board game and chose "Aggravation." Everyone found their seats, and I could see that there was no place on the couch for me, so I sat on the floor next to Evan's feet, and we played the game. Evan won (as he almost always did). We ate and had cake. G opened her presents, and then it was time to get going. I wanted to go to the Saturday Night Life service at Calvary Chapel, and Evan went home. I don't remember what we talked about. I also don't remember if we talked during that next week, but we would see each other again the next weekend.

March 26, Friday. I went to work, happy that it was Friday. I drove straight to Melanie's house to hang out before we went to dinner. Our conversation was monopolized by just who was this man that I brought to the party on Saturday. Melanie and I had been best friends for over ten years, so we talked about everything. Any time I had a problem or needed financial advice or help, she was always my first call. God's sense of humor really showed in His bringing us together as friends. Melanie always had to be doing something, preferably outdoors, and I liked sitting and talking, watching a movie, or just sitting in the quiet. She likes camping and, at the time, I liked my own bed, PERIOD! She would always try to talk me into going camping, and I would always use my "aloneness" as a reason not to. (This worked just fine until, on my wedding day, Melanie's first question was, "When are we going camping?" More about that later.) After dinner, we all went to worship practice and then straight home.

At home, I called Evan, and we talked until after midnight. I was beginning to let my guard down and relax a little. I was also wondering when I would be able to see him again. Hope was stirring.

March 27, Saturday. I slept until I awoke on my own. I loved Saturdays during this time of my life, and I rarely, if ever, made any plans that would require me to wake up early. Evan was away at a function for his daughter, so I spent the day resting, reflecting, and praying about everything. Later I went to Saturday Night Life at Calvary Chapel. This was a weekly service that I had been attending for probably ten years. I used to pick up my youth ministry girls, and we would all go to this service, sitting in the front row, all of us together and singing our hearts out to the Lord. Afterward, we would get something to eat and then go back to my place, where everyone would camp out, like a weekly slumber party, while I was in my own room away from the noise. I lived in a basement apartment, so there were times when the girls were being too loud, and my landlord would give them a few warnings, banging the broom handle on the upstairs kitchen floor, and when that didn't work, he would call my telephone to ask the girls to please quiet down. The fact that they didn't put a stop to the slumber parties altogether just showed how amazing they were. Gradually, the girls would finally calm down and go to sleep, and I would wake them up a few at a time to get ready for Sunday morning church at Centerpoint, where their parents would pick them up and take them home. We did this same routine for over four years, and all but one had graduated from High School. Tonight, though, I was in our usual spot, all alone. I was missing my girls and Evan, but at the same time, I was feeling quite happy and content.

March 28, Sunday. Arriving at Oasis Church, a few people noticed that there was something different about me. You know how people, especially guys, tell each other that they look different, and then say, "You had sex, didn't you?" Of course, I hadn't had sex; I was just happy and a bit giddy. I guess you could say that I was on cloud nine. I was doing my favorite thing in the world, singing to my Lord and Savior, and now I had a new hope of a possible union with a man after God's own heart. When asked what was happening, I was vague about the reason. I hate being teased about things, so I definitely didn't want anyone knowing about Evan (Other than my besties) as God hadn't confirmed everything to either one of us, so it was better to keep things on the DL. After the first service, I left to attend the service at Evan's church, "The Brook." When I arrived, Evan was on stage playing the bass with the worship team. I remember exactly how he looked, wearing a heather grey t-shirt with a black crew neck, black shorts, and flip-flops.

Handsome, very handsome. I sat in the front row, and he joined me after worship was over. There was so much electricity or electromagnetic force between us, and as he sat down, our shoulders touched. I didn't move, even a little, because it could have broken the contact. Oh, and I looked pretty cute, too, in my pink tank top and jeans. I pretended to listen, but all I could hear was the thunder of my heartbeat. After service, I went home, and Evan spent the rest of the day with his family. He wrote a lovely poem of worship before going to sleep that night:

Lord, You know that star I see today
The glimmer of light in the deep blue array
Numerous stars I can faintly see
Are set in place a billion miles from me
Your greatness is so large that there is no empty space
Your greatness so large you can see my face

Rising sun a fresh cool day
Your glory pauses me, I know not what to say
Enjoy! Enjoy! My soul lifts you high
I bask in Your love and stop asking why
Divinely set to fade into night
You'll be with me under a full moonlight

Not a breath from me You haven't known
Evermore I make Your presence known
To and fro I am on the land
Until that day You take my hand
Lift me up to Your great Paradise
I'm longing for You Lord, just to see Your eyes

I bow before You and surrender my will
You fill me with peace and joyful zeal
May Your Spirit fall and fill this man
Your love I'll share impacting all I can
Your blessings are new and You're merciful to me
What today does hold we'll just have to see

March 30, Tuesday. "Adda, you have a call on three."

"Hello?"

"Hi, this is Evan. Would you want to meet me for lunch?"

"Sure. Where should I meet you?"

"How about El Pollo Loco in Redlands?"

"Sure, my lunch is at 11:30."

"Ok, see you there."

We talked over chicken. I have no memory of what we said. He walked me to my car, opened the door for me, and we both went back to work. Later, Evan joined me for my Bible study group. Evan knew everyone in my group because he had previously, and for many years, been a member of Oasis Church. Everyone was happy, however a bit surprised, to see Evan there. He talked about the combined service project between our group and his new group from The Brook, at the Lion's Club, on Saturday and invited everyone over to his house for a BBQ afterward. We sat together on the carpet, and everyone began to sing worship songs and lift up prayers for each other. I could tell that Evan wanted to say something; his forehead was sweating profusely, so I got up and went to the kitchen for some paper towels. I wet them with cold water and handed them to him. He was surprised by the gesture and has mentioned it many times over the years, saying how it blessed him so much and showed him what kind of woman I was. It was such a great night, and Evan became a regular in the group from that time on.

April 2, Friday. My usual Friday was at hand. I couldn't wait to get home that night and call Evan. He told me about a vision that he had, seeing two birds flying across the sky, together, and how beautiful that picture was. And then, he read in Luke 10:1-5 about how God sent the disciples out two by two. Paired up in order to encourage and support each other. If one of them fell, the other would be there to pick him up, and how when two or more are gathered there our God is, in their midst.

April 3, Saturday. My day and evening were completely planned out, including the afternoon BBQ at Evan's house. I drove to the Lion's Club building, and as was usually the case, I did very little of the difficult physical labor and stuck mostly to light duties. I said nothing about Evan or what I was thinking about, but I guess a few people either noticed Evan watching me or were just prompted by God to begin "selling" him to me.

"You know, Evan is the most honest person I know."

"Oh, great, thanks for telling me."

"Miss Adda, other than my husband, Evan is the kindest person that I know."

"Ok, thanks!"

I arrived at Evan's home, and he was outside manning the BBQ while I stayed in the house. I could see him from the window, and I could see and feel him watching me. He sent me a text message: "Do you want cheese on your burger?"

"Why yes, thank you," was my reply.

He actually brought my burger to me (no one else received such service) and dutifully went back outside to continue cooking for everyone. I ate and continued visiting with friends until it was time to leave for church. I let Evan know that I was leaving, and he walked me out to my car. I thanked him for his hospitality (not like that, ha-ha), and he gave me a hug. This was our first real physical contact, and it was the most comforting and protective hug I had ever received. It felt like God, Himself was holding me and reassuring me that this was right. This was what I had asked and longed for, for so many years. I don't even remember going to Calvary Chapel that evening.

April 4, Sunday. I was up early to get ready to go to sound check at church. I felt pretty calm as long as I focused on Jesus and the worship set. Everything went well, and we went into Pastor's office for a group meeting. There was a slight change in the service, and would we want to listen to this song that would be played in the middle of the set? I had never heard the song "Word of God Speak" by Mercy Me, and it was beautiful. Beautiful things often make me cry, so I was crying, and I felt such a vulnerability in my spirit. I was ready for God to speak to me about my future and the love of this man who wanted to pursue me. Unbeknownst to me, Evan was having his own "word of God speak" moment at around midnight that morning. I remained very emotional and decided to go home right after church so that I could talk to Evan about how God had confirmed everything to me. He was excited to give me the details of his own confirmation from God, and we talked for quite a while. I remember sleeping very peacefully that night.

Evan wrote a letter to me very late that evening:

Dearest Love from God,

I write to you under the moonlit sky in the cool April chill. My hand is in shadow and shaking from a heart beating with joy. My insides are shaking, and my mind is racing, thinking of the beauty that I miss. You are flesh of my flesh and bones of my bones. Two weeks have changed my life, and one night has been etched into my memory. We both were filled with His joy and though we were apart, we cried together in complete happiness of the goodness of God.

As I am writing, a bagpipe player is on the cliff playing "Amazing Grace," and if I didn't know better, I would say that Jesus blessed this day. I pause in awe of Him. I'm sitting under a full moon with a bagpipe playing "Amazing Grace" as I am writing to the woman I love. Yes, my spirit overflows with an abundance of love for you. I love that you love Jesus and live for Him. I love the beauty that He has blessed you with, not only inner but outer beauty that surpasses this moon, a flower, and mostly my hopes.

Last night when I reflected on how blessed I am to have my daddy give me permission to take your hand to be with me until death do us part (I would prefer to be raptured together). I love your heart to serve others, your care for people. You amazed me from the very first hour that we spoke. Yes, it is true that we have been acquaintances in church and have also been running into each other at Stater Brothers, and so discovering your parallel life with mine gives me the notion of "two peas in a pod."

How could this be, Lord? I knew how you felt without your telling me. I knew your heart on Saturday by our hug (also etched into my memory). Looking into your eyes brings peace to my soul, and hearing your voice calms my nerves, and I want to run fast into your arms forever. How could this be that the Lord would bless me? Amazing grace is surely what I see.

I know how you feel right now, and I know your answer. (Oh Lord, help me to allow You to lead me in the right timing.) Sorry, just had to lift up a quick prayer.

I love that you worship all day, like me, that you pray without ceasing, like me, and you serve unconditionally, like me. We are so much alike in Jesus Christ that I can only say, the flesh of my flesh and bone of my bone. I feel free as a bird, flying high in the sky as an eagle. I wish I had their night vision right now, it's hard to write under the moonlight. I hope that my tax bill will be small so that I can use the extra money to buy you a ring. Then I will take you to the beach. The perfect spot is the grassy area at the top of Corona Del Mar, where we will watch the sunset and then, before it is gone, I will wash your feet, and as I dry them, I will have the ring wrapped in a cloth. I will pull it out, and words from Heaven will come to my lips.

You will say yes, and we will then have communion together for the first time, right there! Yep, that's how it will be as per my Lord and Savior Jesus Christ. Wow, so much so fast. Yeah, I see the Kingdom of God, and I will sell all that I have to buy it. You, oh Adda, have captured the favor of God, and now He is choosing to bless me with the most wonderful wife a man could ever desire. (Oh Lord, watch over my steps that I may walk in Your perfect will. Never will I say that You have not blessed me because Your face is surely upon me this day.)

My love, I must go rest my hand, for I could write to you all night.

I truly love you, Evan.

April 5, Monday. I had been going to my mom's, at least one night a week, for dinner ever since I had moved out on my own. In 2002, our Monday nights were overtaken by a guy named Jack Bauer. We had just found out about the television show "24" from a friend of my mom's. He said that it was the most exciting show he had ever seen. We decided to try it out. Unfortunately, we had missed all of season one, so we came in at the beginning of season two. We were mesmerized after the first episode, and so my Monday nights at Mom's became "24" and dinner nights. At least we didn't have the same problem that we had when "ER" and "Chicago Hope" premiered and aired at the same time on different networks, but we still couldn't wait for each Monday night to come around so that we could see just what harrowing (and ridiculous) situations Jack would find himself in and how he would save the entire human race from the bad people.

Back to April 5. I'm at my desk, working, and the phone rings. We all took turns answering the phones whenever our receptionist was at lunch, and this time I answered the phone in my usual business-like voice.

"IBF, this is Adda; how can I help you?"

"Hi, this is Evan," he said in a low-key voice that would make a most wonderful radio announcer. "Do you think that your Mom will be really tired tonight and want you to leave early?"

I laughed and assured him that I would be available whether she was tired or not. We would meet at Starbucks, on Hospitality, at 8:00 pm. Why this particular Starbucks, you ask? It was the closest to where I lived, and he didn't want me to drive very far to get home (I know, sweet, huh?). I couldn't focus on my work, so I took lunch and just sat at my desk. I didn't want to eat and I didn't want to talk to anyone. I was filled with an incredible amount of love and hope, but I was also a bit scared. This would be our very first "Date," and I was always bad at dates, especially first ones. I opened up my computer and started typing. Before I knew it, I had written a little love poem. I printed it out to give to him tonight, on our first date. It went like this:

Is this the way it always begins?

Love so sweet and pure

Constant anticipation and longing for this person

Being at a loss for words most of the time (me, not you),

Tired but utterly exhilarated

Safe and so secure but then unsure of all that the future will hold

Does it come from the love for our Lord and Savior?

Are we going too fast? Are there laws or even rules?

Can you love a person so intensely that you actually feel the very love of God?

Can you really know after just three days?

Can I even make it through this day and evening until I see you again?

I did make it through the rest of the work day, and, as predicted, my mom told me that she was very tired and, oh yes, asked, "Could you leave early?" Before I left, Evan and I were texting back and forth, well, flirting was more like it, so I was sitting there after dinner, giggling like a schoolgirl. Mom told me to be careful and to call her when I got home. Of course, I always called Mom when I got home for the night, but this time it was more about wanting to know everything that happened on this "first date."

When I arrived at Starbucks, Evan was already there. He

looked good, of course. He was wearing a black V-neck golf warmer and jeans. He always looked gorgeous, even in his paint clothes. He hugged me and handed me a single pink rose. I'm sure I must have blushed, and then he asked me what I would like to drink. Hmm, not entirely sure, but I probably asked for a decaf mocha frappe. We went inside to order the drinks and out walked Karilee, one of my high school youth group girls (now all grown up). We talked for a minute, and then I sat in a chair facing the door. Evan joined me and said that we should go look at rings. You know, WEDDING RINGS! I just looked at him and said, "Okay." (God had already confirmed, to me and to Evan, that we would get married, so why not look at rings?)

With drinks in hand, we headed to the outdoor tables and sat across from each other. We held hands over the table, and Evan looked at me and said, "Ask me to ask you a question." I was thinking, "Okay, what is this about?" but I found myself just blurting out, "Ask me a question." I know it's cheesy but bear with me. He then said, "Can I kiss you?" I said yes, and we had our first kiss on our first date, the one where he said that we should go and look at rings, and it was perfect. I hadn't been kissed in a long time! It had been twelve years since I had dated anyone (no, I never dated the guy that I made a fool of myself with), so I was not only unsure of myself, but I think I came off a bit wild!

The last thing I remembered was doing a lot of passionate kissing in the parking lot of Starbucks, under the stars, on our first date. I gave him the little love poem that I had written and went home, only to fall asleep. Yeah, I slept like a happy baby. And yeah, I called my mom.

"When do I get to meet him?"

"Soon, Momma, soon."

"Come to the Legion on Friday Night for Karaoke"

"Okay, if he is free."

"Oh, he had better be free!"

"Okay, Momma, we will be there."

April 6, Tuesday. Evan joined us at our bible study group again that night. He arrived a little late, and so there wasn't a place for him at the table beside me, so he sat across the room. After talking as a group for a while, it was time to take communion. I wanted to be with Evan for this, so I got up from my chair and sat on the floor next to his chair, at his feet. For some reason, this had so much significance to him, and it blessed him so much. Because Evan was a ministerial servant, he wasn't used to people doing things for him. A humble gesture like this one speaks of the heart of a person, and indeed, I couldn't wait to become his wife so that I could use my gift of service for him. We took communion together for the first time—a precious memory for both of us. After communion, we started worshipping, and as we sang, our voices harmonized together, and we knew that it must have been such a sweet sound to our Lord. Our lives would be spent living in harmony with each other as we lived for Jesus and would find ways to serve Him as a couple.

April 7, Wednesday. In the mornings, when I was ready for work, I would sit and have my coffee and my reading time with God. This particular morning, I also wrote a little love letter to my new and very human muse. It went like this:

Dearest,

I am completely enamored by you

Your love for the Lord

The way that you put other people's needs before your own,

Your gentle and playful spirit

Your gift for words

Your love for the Lord

Your servant's heart

The way that we harmonize

Your laugh, it's wonderful

The way that your eyes change color

The kind of father that you are

That you honor your commitments

Your love for the Lord

The way that you turn my flaws into blessings

Your unconditional love

You never complain... about anything

Our compatibility

Your love for the Lord

Later that day, I was working at my desk, and my co-worker and friend Bekky came up to me and said, "Hey Adda, there's a hot guy asking for you upfront."

Hmm, I guess I hadn't mentioned Evan to anyone at work yet, so it would be a very big surprise for a hot guy to show up asking for ME! The proverbial cat was out of the bag, and I would be interrogated upon my return from my little mini-date.

Evan drove us to a coffee shop, and I ordered an Italian Soda, and he ordered coffee (how do I even remember this stuff after almost twenty years?!) We talked over drinks about some life things, his schedule, and mine, and of course, if he was free on Friday night so that he could meet my mom. (More like, are you free to have a bunch of people who love me give you the once over?)

"I'll have to get back to you on that."

He dropped me back at work, and I didn't even get halfway through the door when the questions started flying. Who is he? Where did you meet him? What's he like? (Oh, you mean besides hot?) What does he do for a living? (Uh, he was in his paint clothes when he picked me up.)

After work, I met Evan at his house, and we left for Riverside with Miss Ashley in tow to meet Evan's Mom, Janice, and his sister, Elaine, at a sushi restaurant. We had a wonderful time laughing and getting to know each other. You know, for some people, this is the hardest part, but Evan's family was so accepting and loving that it became easy, and I also loved spending time getting to know Ashley better.

We even talked about the fact that I didn't plan on invading her home and taking over or trying to become a mom to her. She already had a mom. We would figure it out and try to keep communication open and honest. I gave Evan his love letter before we parted for the long, long night until we could see each other the next day. (Don't throw up, it was torturous!)

April 9, Good Friday. Our boss, Craig, blessed all of us with a half-work day for Easter weekend. I was so excited because I was going to meet Evan and Ashley, go to lunch, and just hang out until worship practice. Evan accompanied me and stayed the whole time. After practice was over, we headed to the American Legion Post 106, where my mom worked the day shift and would now be having fun with her friends and boyfriend, Art. Evan wasn't nervous at all; neither was I. I knew that everyone would love Evan immediately. We walked in and found Mom; she whispered in my ear, "He's HOT," and we laughed.

I introduced them, and he got a kiss on the cheek from the most wonderful person on earth (that would be my mother), and they hit it off just like I knew that they would. It was fun introducing Evan to all of Mom's peeps. Mom had worked at this particular job for over twenty years, so I knew pretty much everyone. Mom had just started singing Karaoke songs, so she did one for us, "I'm Not in Love," which was funny because she and I both were very much in love with our guys.

Evan ordered us both a Sprite, and we stayed until about 11:00 pm then Evan took me home. He parked his truck in front of the big trash bin, and we kissed in the moonlight, not caring about the view. (We still joke about going and making out in front of a trash can.). We met the next day to go to Ashley's dance competition. I couldn't wait to see her dance, nor could I wait to see her dad again.

April 10, Saturday. Drove to Evan's house to join them for Ashley's competition day. She was nervous but looked absolutely stunning with her hair, makeup, and costume. She was part of a group jazz dance, and they danced to the song "Beautiful People" by Marilyn Manson. It was an awful song, but the dance was amazing! Every young lady on that stage danced to perfection. We enjoyed the rest of the competition, and I had to hold back tears when a trio performed a dance to one of my favorite songs, "Tiny Dancer." Such a blessing to be part of something so important to Ashley and to spend valuable time with her. She would have to endure just as much of a transition as I would, probably even more.

We had early dinner plans with Evan's friends, Eddie and Nancy, at Mimi's Cafe. I had never eaten there before, so I was excited to try something new. We waited in the parking lot, and according to Nancy, we were doing some making out next to Evan's truck when they arrived. The Boyds were gracious and friendly. I liked them immediately.

I did my usual Meg Ryan impersonation while ordering my food. "Please don't salt anything and all sauces and dressings on the side." I believe I had a very bland meal of grilled chicken and jasmine rice, but the company was anything but bland. After dinner, Evan and I went to Calvary Chapel for the Saturday Night Life service. We ended our wonderful day together doing what we both loved the most, worshipping and praising our Lord and Savior Jesus.

April 11, Sunday. Went to Oasis for church. It was a typical, wonderful Sunday. Completely unexpected was Evan and Ash showing up for the second service!

I felt so much love, and I couldn't remember ever being so happy. One of my biggest "gripes" about being single was not having a significant other to sit in church with. Sitting with friends was great, but as my best friends were all married and had their person, I was still alone and felt it most when at church. Now I felt overjoyed sitting with these two very special ones in my favorite place.

After church, we went to Gina and Mike's for a BBQ and hang-out time. At one point, I looked up from the living room and saw Mike and Chuck glaring at Evan as he caressed me.

It made me laugh but also made me grateful for my friends who felt so protective of me. God has really blessed me, over the years, with amazing friends who I really consider family. It makes me think of Proverbs 18:24, "A man of many companions may come to ruin, but there is a friend who stays closer than a brother." To have such friends is a great blessing indeed.

April 12, Monday. Evan met me at IBF, and we prayed together before work. The work hours seemed long. Lunchtime finally arrived, and I sat at my desk thinking about my new love and the wonderful weekend we spent together.

After work, I drove over to Dance Dimensions to see Evan (to give him the love poem that I wrote for him) and Ashley for a few minutes before heading over to Mom's to have dinner and enjoy more Jack Bauer escapades. My heart was full.

April 13, Tuesday. Work went by slowly, but as soon as I got free, I went over to Evan's to hang out, then to a little Chinese place for a quick dinner, and finally over to Glenn and Carolyn's for our ACTS group.

Evan was given a special prophetic prayer for someone in the group, and I was able to see, probably for the first time, how God would be using us, as a team, to minister to others. Nothing was of more importance to either one of us than fulfilling the purpose of our coming together as a couple. We were both experienced in many types of ministry, but now everything was new, and each opportunity would bring us closer to God, other people, and each other.

I still believe that there is nothing more important than whatever mission God has put before us. Even today, our mission is evident, and we are excited to see what God will do in our new little neighborhood here in Hoquiam, Washington. More about that later.

April 14, Wednesday. Excited from the happenings the night before, I woke up early and spent time praying and reading. I also wrote Evan a quick note:

I want you to know how truly blessed I feel and how excited I am about what God is going to do in our lives and through us as a couple. All things must be in place for you in order for God to pour out His complete blessing upon you and show you what your mission is. It's easy for me because I already know my mission is to love and support YOU! What a cushy assignment! I'm so thankful to Him for everything. My cup overflows! I NEVER KNEW WHAT THAT MEANT UNTIL RIGHT NOW! I Love You.

Evan met me at work again that morning to pray with me, and I gave him his letter before we parted for the day. I saw him briefly before he and Ashley headed to The Brook for practice, and I went to the gym for a relaxing swim before heading home for an early night in. It had been a few weeks since I had been home before

10:00 pm. Nothing but sweet dreams for this girl who was head over heels. Nothing could mess up this euphoric time, except…

April 15, Thursday. Woke up with a terrible "pulling" sensation in my neck. I was pretty sure of the causation for it. Until just recently, I was plagued by constant vertigo. They called it Menier's, and there was no real cure for it. It began about ten years prior, with a strange sound, like holding a sea shell up to your ear, that lasted for about a week. It went away and didn't occur again until the next year, coming in the same sort of way, except this time, it lasted for several weeks.

The next occurrence was much more drastic, as it came with a loud ringing in my ear followed by dizziness that I hadn't felt since the time I had gone on the Tilt a Whirl ride many years before. The scary part was that it happened as I was in my car, pulling out of the driveway. I was barely able to get my car back to my apartment and get myself inside the house when I violently vomited for an hour.

I called Melanie, and she brought me over some Benadryl and stayed with me until I felt better. I took double doses of Benadryl for the next few weeks, and then it went away again.

By 2003 it was so bad that I had at least one occurrence of full-on vertigo every day for over a year. One of the only ways to feel relief was to turn one's head in the opposite direction of the affected ear. So this whole past year, I was basically holding my head, leaning toward the right (left ear was the one affected) while I slept, showered, got ready for work, drove to work, worked at my desk, etc.

I had gone to see several doctors that year, trying to find relief. The last one, in mid-February, a surgeon told me of the procedure that would have him surgically severing the nerve in my left ear, which would help with keeping equilibrium steady.

By doing this, the body would eventually regulate itself back to "normal." However, there were chances that the procedure might cause total deafness in the affected ear, and the recovery would be difficult and not fully guaranteed.

At this point, I was miserable and willing to do anything, even something as drastic and scary as this. There was one caveat—all of his patients had to take a diuretic medication and follow an extremely low sodium diet for six months. Again, I was willing to try anything, so I left with a prescription and a food diary to keep track of my sodium intake. I lived on a minuscule amount of bland food and occasionally "saved up all of my milligrams" so that I could have my favorite Salsa Verde Doritos or a sourdough burger from Carl's JR. for dinner. I started feeling better and also lost all of the 20 pounds that I had gained from taking so much meclizine that I could knock out a lion with it.

By this time, I was able to get through most days without a full-blown attack, so I guess I was holding my head back to a normal angle which was causing this pulling sensation in my neck. I called my friend Zita who worked for a chiropractor, and made an appointment for some x-rays. They confirmed my suspicion-my neck now had a curve, and the muscle and tendons were being pulled and stretched trying to get back to normal. I would need a whole series of visits and adjustments to get me back to health.

My boss heard about this and offered to loan me the funds to pay upfront, which saved a lot of money in the long run. I accepted his offer, and Evan took me to almost all of my appointments and never once told me to suck it up when I would be crying from the pain of the adjustment. I was given my first adjustment and went home right afterward to rest. I still HATE the feeling of chiropractic adjustments to this day.

Back to April 15. It was really hard to focus on work; however, a printing brokerage is almost always extremely busy with orders coming in, placing those orders, follow-ups with vendors, invoicing jobs, discussing new clients, handling the problems with orders—there were always problems, and filing all of the paperwork (always my LEAST favorite part of any office position. Hmm, I don't enjoy putting away the clean dishes, folding and putting away of the laundry, or taking out the trash either).

During lunch, I called Evan and then wrote him a little love poem:

Man, after God's own heart, you have already captured mine

Kissing me with the kisses of your mouth, your love truly is sweeter than wine

Greater love never have I known, nor better purpose for my love which has waited so long to be shown

Amazing love so few can understand, having been molded and crafted by our wonderful Father's hands

Neither lavish gifts nor poetic words are required to love you with a heart that is truly on fire

For you reflect the love of Jesus who said that it is finished, this love that I have for you never will diminish

April 16, Friday. I couldn't wait to get finished at work so that I could start my weekend with my love. I left at five o'clock, on the nose, and raced over to Evan's, where Ashley was making us dinner. At fifteen, she was already an accomplished cook, and we relaxed and watched a program on TV. (I laugh as I write this because, after nineteen years together, I know that the only thing that kept Evan awake as we waited for dinner was his own excitement about our future together. He is always falling asleep on the couch.)

We discussed a few possible wedding dates and then enjoyed our time with Ashley and, of course, the meal. Then we went to Oasis for worship practice. Evan took me there, and once again, he stayed with me the whole time.

Pastor Steve was there late, so I ran into his office to tell him all that had happened. For the past four years, he had counseled and comforted me in my singleness and desire to marry. One time he told me to remember that you cannot put new wine into old wineskins (Reference Luke 5: 37-39). The biblical reference was not at all about marriage, but I understood Pastor's meaning by it. I reflected on that passage of scripture for a long time, a year perhaps, praying and thinking about what changes I needed to make in order to become a new wineskin, one worthy of the man God had chosen for me. I had no idea about the who or the when, but I did know that he would be an amazing man of God, a man after God's heart. One of the things that God showed me was that I needed to learn how to keep my opinions to myself unless someone asked. Before learning this lesson, I would literally walk up to someone who I knew was having troubles and tell them what they needed to do or fix in order for things to get better.

Imagine that you are just hanging out somewhere, and a person walks up to you and says, "You know, if you would just do this or stop doing that, your life would get a lot easier!" Yes, I did that, and I did it all the time. Sometimes perfect strangers were subject to my interference. I thought that I was helping them.

I knew that when something was wrong in my life, I needed to stop doing something or stop fighting whatever I thought was wrong. But my approach doesn't even work for me all of the time, so why did I think that other people would benefit from it?

I tried to recall how I started this behavior, and truly, I believe that it started when I was very young. I had deep emotional hurt, and I didn't want to talk about it with anyone. I tried to pretend like I was happy but kept all of the bad feelings hidden. Since then, I started looking for problems in other people's lives and tried to fix them. I believe this trait is called "Codependency."

I wasn't aware of the term, but God showed me that I needed to start talking about my own feelings and get some healing, or I wouldn't make a very good partner in life. That other person would be under constant scrutiny and would be pretty miserable. Did I really want to marry someone only to make them miserable? No, just the opposite. I wanted to be a constant source of blessing and encouragement for people, especially for my spouse. I had a lot of learning and unlearning to do. I stopped interfering with other people's lives and started focusing on my own self. Prayer and a lot of reading about the God kind of love that would be uplifting to people, not tearing them down, was required, and it took time; it always takes time to become something new.

I still struggle with trying to solve every problem that I see in other people, but I have come a long way in these past twenty or so years. With God, it really is possible to change and to change for the betterment of everyone, not just myself.

We ended the evening with a talk at Starbucks, where we ran into another one of my girls, Holly, who got to meet Evan and snapped a photo of us before leaving. We talked over coffee about the plans for the weekend. We talked about God. We always talked about God.

April 17, Saturday. My Uncle Bill and Aunt Nita were pastors of a little church called "Come as You Are." Many amazing things happened during their tenure there, but a few really stand out. I was baptized in the Holy Spirit there, and I was also miraculously healed on another occasion. It's funny that without the latter, I would never have spent so much time ministering to young people, and I certainly wouldn't be in a relationship with Evan.

It was the summer of 1995. I had three guy friends that I hung out with a lot, and one was the worship leader at my Uncle's church. His name was Paul. On a Saturday afternoon, we went to the church for what my Uncle called a "revival meeting."

Uncle Bill introduced a man from Sacramento, I believe, and said that he was a prophet and healer. I don't remember his name since we weren't properly introduced.

During the "greeting" time, this prophet man walked up to me and said, "God wants to heal you from your smoking addiction." I told him, "No, thank you," and went and sat down with my worship leader friend. He asked me, "What did the man say to you?" I answered, "He told me that God wanted to heal me from smoking, and I told him no thank you." Paul incredulously asked me, "Then what are you doing sitting here?!" I replied, "I like my cigarettes, thank you very much!" He didn't say anything else. He just grabbed my hand and led me over to the prophet man. He and other people prayed for me for over three hours. Someone even prayed that I wouldn't gain any weight after I stopped smoking.

As God is my witness, as well as all of the other people

involved, I walked out of that meeting as a non-smoker. I have never craved a cigarette, and it's been over twenty-five years. Praise God!

The fact that Evan hates cigarettes and would have thought twice about being with me if my addiction had continued was just another part of the miracle that happened that day.

Not to mention the twenty-plus years that I spent ministering and mentoring young people would not have been possible had I continued to smoke. Now, if I could only hate sweets as much as cigarettes…..

Back to April 17 and my Uncle and Aunt's church. I was on my way to the church for their monthly meeting called "Beauty for Ashes." They created it for the women in the community to gather, share a meal, and be encouraged. I attended whenever I could, and this particular Saturday, Evan stopped by to meet them and some of the other ladies at the meeting. He was charming, as usual, and had them all eating out of his hand, so to speak. One of the ladies asked him, "Are you He?" and he said, pointing toward Heaven, "No, HE is He. I'm just me."

All I could do was smile and thank God for all of the things that led up to this moment and for the things that were yet to come.

After the meeting, I drove to Evan's house, and we took off to the mall and Kay's Jewelers there. Evan pointed out a lovely round diamond in a gold setting, and it was beautiful, but I felt that it was a bit too big for my small hands. Besides, I prefer silver settings and marquise-cut diamonds.

The attendant led me to a case where I saw a beautiful ¼ Ct marquise diamond in a platinum setting. It was, indeed, a flawless internal diamond, and did it sparkle! It was a much better diamond than the other ½ Ct one and at a better price too.

Most men would expect the bride-to-be to desire a bigger diamond, but there is much to be said about the quality of the diamond and its enduring value. When we visited the store, years later, to have my wedding set resized, they offered us four thousand dollars for the set, and we hadn't even paid half that much.

In the past, I have lost many rings for various reasons, which is why now I never remove my rings except to clean them. In eighteen years, there would have been plenty of opportunities to misplace or lose them entirely.

Back to Saturday, again. We left the mall and headed to our already favorite sushi bar for dinner before the Saturday Night Life service at Calvary Redlands. I was surprised to see one of my former co-workers at the service. We said our hellos, and I introduced him to Evan (I'm trying to remember if he was able to attend our wedding). I remember him fondly and always hoped that he would be able to find a good wife and have some kids. He would certainly make a fine husband and father.

It had been a very wonderful and busy day. We said goodnight, and I drove home feeling euphoric. God was blessing me more than I could have imagined, and believe me, I did a great deal of imagining during my long tenure as a single.

When you're older and single, a kind of hopelessness can overtake you, and you can lose your zest for life. You can wake up asking yourself, "Why should I even get up and go through the motions if this is as good as it will ever get?"

When people tell you to relax, God's timing is perfect, or that

He works all things for the good of those who love him, you just want to smack them.

One thing that always kept me going was just remembering that God is perfect and He never changes. He always keeps His promises, and He really does work all things in my life together for my ultimate good. Had I not continued to trust Him, even when I was unhappy, I would have never received my most wonderful blessing, Evan Roy Dahlke.

April 18, Sunday. Sunday has been my favorite day of the week ever since I gave my heart to Jesus back in 1983, and this day was no exception. I couldn't wait to see everyone and get all of my hugs.

I sent Evan a text, "I love you SO much!" and headed to Oasis. Evan arrived just before the second service started, and again, I was so happy to be in God's house with the man I loved.

We went to lunch and then furniture shopping. Strange that we would go furniture shopping when we had two already furnished homes, but Evan wanted to have at least new bedroom furniture in place for our new beginning. We decided to hold off on purchasing anything as it wasn't a necessity to have new things, and Evan said that God makes all things new anyway.

We finished the day with a dinner at La Cabana with Pastor Dane, Senior Pastor of Colton First Baptist Church. I had e-mailed Pastor Dane a few days earlier about Evan and that I wanted them to meet.

Dane has been my Pastor since I moved to Southern California in 1985. I'll never forget my first day at CFB. I had driven by the church on my way home from the grocery store. I liked the way the building looked, it had many stained glass windows, and I decided to visit the next Sunday. I walked up the stairs on that first morning, and there was an adorable lady at the door greeting everyone who came in. Her name was Elsie Lamb, and she hugged me as I walked in and told me how glad she was to see me. I asked her where the Sunday school class was, and when I walked in, a young man greeted me and said, "Hi, I'm Dane Aaker, and I'm the Senior Pastor here." My first thought was, "You're kidding, right?" because he was so young, around 28, and I knew that this was an old church with an older congregation.

He and his wife, Karen, have been a source of wisdom, teaching, and support to me my entire adult life. Evan was impressed by Dane, and I believe he decided that very evening that he wanted to be mentored by Dane in the future. We attended CFB and had a wonderful time worshipping and hearing Pastor Dane teach.

Parting was always such sweet sorrow when we had to say goodnight till it be morrow.

April 19, Monday. Went to work, knowing that I wouldn't see Evan at all that day. He was going to be working late and then had a family situation to deal with the same evening, and I would be at my Mom's for dinner.

I wrote this during lunch:

A heavy heart whose beloved is elsewhere

Cannot write about love today

NOTE: When I decided to write this memoir, I started out by making a timeline of our whirlwind relationship. I was having a lot of trouble remembering details, so Evan offered me his journals to fill in the blanks. I asked him if he was sure, and he said yes. In fact, he said that I could read all of them, not just the ones pertaining to our meeting and subsequent marriage. I spent two weeks reading them all, dating back to 2003 and ending in 2017 when he began an altogether different form of journaling. What a blessing this was for me! Not only helping with the timeline but opening up such a treasure trove of situations and circumstances that sparked my memory and gave me so much more to share about. At this point, there are some gaps between entries, so I will skip to days when I have some details; after all, this stuff happened almost twenty years ago, and these days it can be challenging just to remember what happened yesterday, let alone things from many years ago. I will share the love poems that I wrote since they do include the dates that I wrote them on.

April 20, Tuesday.

Why Do I Love You? Twelve Reasons

1. *You love the Lord*

2. *You Love Your Neighbor as Yourself*

3. *You Trust Him*

4. *Our First Kiss*

5. *Goofy Moments*

6. *Your Heart Pursues Righteousness*

7. *Your Romantic Spirit*

8.   *Our Balance*

9.   *You Love to Worship Jesus*

10. *Purity*

11. *You Chose ME*

12. *Twelve Roses*

April 2004

(Not sure about the meaning of number 12. I can guess, though. It probably means that Evan gave me roses on or about the twelfth day of our romance, one for every day. It sounds like something he would do.)

April 21st, Wednesday.

I miss you more today than the day before

So great is my anticipation to see you each morning to pray with you, to kiss you

Then, I am forced to leave you again!

Oh, the misery!

I count the minutes

Slowly they pass by

Slowly I wait

Always waiting!

April 22, Thursday.

I can't get enough of you

Never want to leave you

Never want to stop holding you

Never tire of hearing you say my name

Absolutely never want to stop kissing you!

More in love with you every day or maybe even every minute

Long goodbyes are a favorite time

There will be a day when we will have to say goodbye no longer

My love for you will be even stronger when we become one

I will still never get enough of you

April 23, Friday.

Blow, Wind of Change, Blow!

Make us FLY as on eagle's wings!

Let our voices of worship rise up to sing!

Glory to God in the highest!

(Not sure what happened to inspire this. Evan does not have a journal entry for this or the previous day).

April 24, Saturday. Ashley had a dance competition out of town, so I didn't see Evan until that evening. We met at Mimi's for dinner, and we decided on a date for our wedding, June 27, a Sunday.

We thought it would be fun to have our wedding in a park setting with a picnic lunch after all of the church services were finished, around noon. People could show up, at their leisure, with the actual ceremony to begin at 2:00 pm. Evan would try to sell his jet-skies and a few other things to pay for the bulk of the wedding. I would get my dress and have the invitations printed through my work. As we sat in front of our trash can for a while before Evan went home, we decided to work out other details on another day.

June 27 seemed so far away. I know it was only two months away, and we had a whole wedding to plan and prepare for.

April 27, Tuesday.

I love Your mercy, oh Lord
New every morning and lovely all throughout the day,
I cast my cares upon You and rest in Your presence
You give me constant peace and extend to me your grace.

I have heard the Good News and have seen Your ways
I want to shout it from the rooftops!
I want to dance as David danced!
Make my voice, oh Lord, one of continuous praise!

Extend to the man of my dreams Your hand of kindness
Cause him to see Your amazing love for him
Set his heart to beat with Yours
Bind our will to Yours and give to us the mind of Christ

Let us not sin against You but bring You glory
Let our hearts not be troubled as we trust in You
Your perfect timing
Your perfect will
Your everlasting goodness

April 30, Friday.

Your love fills my heart with joy

It makes my spirit soar

Lifts my countenance to a higher place

You're so protective, conquering all of my fears

Giving me a glimpse of the AMAZING love of God

May 3, Monday. Evan's Birthday. I am not sure what we did or if I was involved in his birthday celebration. No journal entries until May 16. I wrote to him almost daily, though, during that time:

Loving you brings glory to God and purpose for me

I live for the joy of each opportunity to encourage you, bless you, and lift your spirits

To be your helper is my role

To finish well in everything I do for you is my goal

May 5th, Wednesday.

There is a place called Heaven that I have always read and dreamt about yet never really understood. Now that my life on earth feels a lot like heaven, I have a better idea of what it will actually be like. I had never known this kind of earthly joy and happiness until I met you.

I have always felt that I needed to feel the love of the Father, and now it is being manifested, physically, through you.

When I am weak, you are strong, and I can now better accept my weaknesses.

When I'm tired from the heat of the day, you are like a fresh cool breeze, there to refresh me.

When I feel overwhelmed by life, I need only tell you and I have your help as well as your loving arms to hold and comfort me.

My account has been credited for my many years of waiting, so now my cup is running over, my sorrows have been turned to joy, and my mourning has been turned into dancing.

May 6th, Thursday.

You live inside my heart, sitting at the feet of Jesus

Occupying my dreams, right in tune with the Spirit's direction

Love surrounding me, like waves in the ocean

My thoughts go from Jesus to you, you to Jesus, like verse and chorus

Beautiful melodies playing in my head

ξ

He's a breath of fresh air-sweet, funny and charming

Every woman's dream but only this girl's reality

Most blessed among women am I, everyone agrees

I gladly give up everything, forever with him to cleave

May 7, Friday.

You melt my heart, you really do

I need only look into your amazing green eyes to be completely undone

All my inhibitions have gone away, I DID have them, you know

Deep insecurities and loathing of self

Wondering if I could ever be loved just for being a woman after God's heart

Knowing now that this is why you have chosen me fills my heart with joy

That surpasses all understanding and reason

May 11, Tuesday.

As my heart yearns to worship the Lord, it also yearns for you

As much as I desire to please Him, I also desire to please you

As the trees long for the rain, my soul longs for you

As many are the stars in the sky are my many thoughts I think toward you

As much as I need oxygen to live, I need you to have complete joy

May 12, Wednesday.

I know that you will still love me, even after the honeymoon is over

When you find out that I'm really a pain and very opinionated

When I whine about having to work or do the laundry

On days that I wake up with a frown

When I have more gray hair than brown

I know that you will still love me

Because I will ALWAYS be in love with you

May 15, Saturday. Made an appointment at David's Bridal, and Melanie and I went to find my wedding dress. You may be wondering why I was looking for my wedding dress before I was even engaged or after knowing this man for only a few months, but we were both so sure of our future, and even the naysayers had to admit that it all seemed right. I was so excited to find my dress. I have always preferred simple yet elegant styles, and I found four dresses right away that appealed to me. I had also lost about 20 pounds from doing the low sodium diet and my doctor has prescribed so my confidence level was high .

The first dress that I tried on was a chiffon with a deep V-Neck that just hung on me. I don't really think outside the box or see what things COULD be after improvement, so I cast this choice off very quickly. The second dress was form-fitting with a long train and lace and pearl off shoulder cap sleeves. As soon as it was all fastened, I knew that this was the one. I showed Mel, and she liked it too. The attendant told me that I would need a few alterations, so I needed to get on the waiting list. I asked her how long the wait would be, and she said about six months. Uh, six months would put us into November, and we had already decided on June 27, a little over a month away.

I was stressed, so I called Evan, and he told me that one of his clients was a seamstress and he would call her and ask if she could do the alterations for me.

She said yes, so I purchased the dress and met Evan at his place so we could go to his client's house with the dress. Her name was Rose. She took all the measurements and said that she could have it done in a few weeks. Whew, that made my life a whole lot easier. It's funny how I still get stressed out about things, and Evan will still come alongside me and help solve the problems without me even asking.

He is such a great problem-solver.

May 16, Sunday. Our favorite day of the week was spent with our favorite people. After worship services, we all went to Chuck and Melanie's for a BBQ. Weather-wise, it was a lovely day. We had a badminton tournament (which I did NOT participate in), and Evan got to show off some more of his skills. There was such ease in being with these people that Evan quickly became one of the gang and was already bantering, especially with Gina. They were like brother and sister and had the rest of us laughing at their antics. We concluded the day with a round of Aggravation with Evan, again showing his ultra-competitive side. We said our goodbyes and then headed over to my little place to watch a movie. Poor Evan; he said that he wanted to watch all of my favorites but really didn't know what he was getting into.

That night we watched "It Could Happen to You," a cute romantic comedy about a cop who didn't have a tip for the waitress but promised that if he won the lottery with the ticket that he had just purchased, he would split it with her. Evan really HAS watched all of the movies that I had at the time. He never complained about any of them, however, he does refuse to watch some of them for a second time. Some would say that our romance was just as cheesy as the one depicted in this movie and, for that matter, MOST romantic comedies. I happen to believe that ours is just as fun and, most of the time, as light-hearted as all of my favorites.

May 17, Monday. This was going to be a very long week!

We were leaving on Friday, after work, for the airport and then flying to San Francisco to meet Evan's brother Aaron and his wife Liane, who lived in Seattle, Washington. I would first have to get through a whole week of anticipation for my first trip, anywhere, in a very long time. I don't travel well, so I wasn't looking forward to the flying part, but I was so excited to see this ultra-famous city with its beautiful Victorian architecture—especially the Painted Ladies and Haight-Ashbury—and, of course, the Golden Gate Bridge. There was also a lighthouse, and I LOVE lighthouses. I had purchased a particular dress for our romantic evening out and also a leather jacket to keep me warm. I was still writing little love notes, almost daily, and giving them to him.

My love for you is not like a whirlwind (there's that word again) or a tornado

Those are usually violent and destructive.

I compare our love to the beautiful love of God.

It has no beginning or end...it has just always been

May 18, Tuesday.

You have the softest heart… you really do

Taking on hostile situations, calming the storms.

You champion the needy while the rest stand in awe.

Always seeing the best in people, you have received the Father's call

May 20th, Thursday.

My beloved is like a garden; he awakens many of the senses and is very beautiful

He is like an ocean wave, unstoppable by human might

His love is like the love of God, unchanging and unconditional

His voice is like an angel's, whispering the Truth in my ear

May 21, Friday. Talk about the longest workday/week in history! I literally ran to my truck and drove home to feed my cat and gather my things for the trip. Evan helped me to the truck. We drove to the Ontario Airport, parked in short-term parking, and headed to the terminal. Clearing security took a bit longer due to the September 11 attacks that had occurred just a couple of years before. Evan had a very difficult few days, so he was a bit on edge at first, but he quickly changed channels, and now we were on our way to having a lovely weekend. We didn't get to our hotel until 11:30 pm. I had my own room, of course, and it was beautiful. This was an expensive hotel, and it was only my second or third time staying in any hotel. Evan was staying in a suite with his brother and wife, sleeping on the hide-a-bed in the living room.

Aaron pulled out a whiteboard to go over our agenda for the next few days. At that time, I thought this was a bit strange, but now that I know his brother, this was just how they did things, and I appreciated it since I like to have a plan with everything decided on. Evan, of course, is the opposite. He likes things to be played out in a spontaneous manner, not knowing absolutely what is coming next. We would have breakfast followed by a trip to the botanical gardens, then lunch at Pier 39 so that the guys could get their clam chowder bread bowls, and we could see some of the many shops and peculiar people in the area. I went to sleep feeling euphoric. Of course, I would have to rise a bit earlier than my usual Saturday. The gang wasn't going to wait until 10:00 for breakfast.

May 22, Saturday. Woke up at 6:00 am to get ready for the day. At this particular time in life, I awoke early every work day and on Sunday in order to shower and wash my hair, apply full makeup, dry and style my hair, etc., which took about ninety minutes! I can't even imagine doing all of that every single day now. More on how Evan convinced me to change this, later.

We ate breakfast at the hotel and headed to the Botanical Gardens, a paradise in the heart of Golden Gate Park. There are over 50 acres filled with thousands of types of flora. It is also a pretty common location for wedding proposals, but I was still thinking of the beautiful red dress that I would wear that evening for Evan's proposal. After our tour, we spent some time walking around at Pier 39, where the guys, indeed, got clam chowder bread bowls while Liane and I chose some fresh smoked fish with bread and whipped butter. I loved the shops with all of the souvenirs, and I picked up a San Francisco shot glass for Mom. There were so many shirts, hats, beach towels… you name it. It was all so colorful. I also bought a pink baseball cap with San Francisco embroidered on it, and I still have it.

The next destination was across the Golden Gate Bridge to Point Bonita Lighthouse. It had gotten pretty windy, and we had to walk half a mile through the tunnel to get to the suspension bridge and then across to the lighthouse. I neglected to bring a hair tie or scarf, so my hair was flying EVERYWHERE in the 25 MPH wind.

There was a bench near the lighthouse, and I wanted to sit and rest for a bit. As I sat down, Evan got on one knee and took a purple towel out, which was embroidered with our names and our wedding date, June 27. In it was wrapped a tiny ring, the one that we had picked out, and he placed it on my finger and asked me to be his bride. I said yes, of course, and then he started to remove my shoes so that he could wash my feet and dry them with the towel. We then took communion together with Aaron and Liane, and they prayed over us, asking God to bless our union and use us mightily as a couple. Well, that was unexpected!! (Evan is especially adorable when he has a secret to keep. He so wants to tell me, and he is giddy with the anticipation of my reactions.) We decided to go to Bubba Gump's for dinner, not heading back to the hotel to change, but that was alright.

The little red dress was forgotten as we laughed and ate our meals with gusto. We were exhausted when we got back to the hotel. I retired to my room to call Mom and reflect on the amazing day filled with beauty and so much love.

May 23, Sunday. After breakfast, we headed to the airport for the flight home.

I was thirty-nine years old, and this had been my first real trip to a famous city. It was also my first marriage proposal or engagement. When I turned thirty-six, I had decided that my childbearing days were behind me and that I would not be having children. I was sad. I had always wanted to have children and be a mom. Melanie told me once that if I had kids, they would never get to do anything, but they would be loved.

HA-HA! God knew that I would be a control freak and probably make their lives miserable, so he spared the children. Now, at 39, I knew that my little prophetic moment was right. Evan was not able to have more children, so there you have it. Later on, I really prayed that I would get pregnant. I told Evan, and we both prayed for it. When I look back, I think that I wanted a child to come so as to stop all of the madness that was going on in my life. All of the things that I couldn't control because I wasn't using my voice. More about that later.

We landed, and Evan took me home. I wrote him a letter that night:

Dearest,

This weekend was the very best of my life, not because of the beauty of the sea, trees, and gardens or the food and fellowship with your family, who are now my friends. All of these make for good times and long-lasting memories, but what I really loved about this weekend was that every waking hour was spent with you, the man that I love and cherish. Your proposal was genuine, original, and filled with so much love and humility. You promised to love me as Christ loved the church, giving himself up for her. When you washed my feet, you said that it meant that you would always take care of me. I know that you will keep these promises—

there are so few men who know and accept their role as husbands. If the woman is indeed the weaker sex, then she needs to be cherished and cared for. Every time I have been in a state of weakness or stress, you have been there to help and support me, offering solutions to problems or just a hug to comfort me. God really knew which pot to put this fragile flower into. I am so blessed to have you. I also love that you promised to give me the letter that you wrote to me on April 4. I remember that day so well. If you wish, I will give you the letter that I wrote to the Lord that very same day.

I love you with all of my heart.

NOTE: Neither of us journaled anything for almost a month after this. I have letters from both of us, but nothing else until June 16, the day that we had my dress fitting and our primary wedding photos taken.

May 25th, Tuesday.

I am the pleasantly passionate and peaceful lover of your soul. I like this title.

I love you

I pray that I bring you nothing but peace, joy, and so much love

I love and accept you for the person that you are

You can be as goofy as you want to be, romantic as often as you like, serious, or procrastinating... I love every aspect of you

Go ahead, challenge me... my love will remain the same

It comes from the heart of the Father, who IS love and never changes

May 26th, Wednesday.

You know that you're in love when you count the minutes until you see your beloved again

You know that you're in love when you don't care that you're dog tired

You know that you're in love when your time with the Lord is interrupted, and you're still filled with joy

You know that you're in love when you see your beloved from across the room, and your heart leaps within you

You know that you're in love when all of your thoughts and dreams about the future include your beloved

You know that you're in love when you have finally been chosen, and you can say with your whole heart, YES

I know that I'm in love

June 7, Monday. Our wedding invitations came in, and they were perfect. I went over to Evan's, and we finalized our guest list. I addressed all of the envelopes, 250 of them, while Evan and Ashley stuffed the invitations and attached the postage. Ashley also made us a very nice dinner, and we had a wonderful evening. We went to find her a dress later in the week. She would be our "flower girl," Evan's brother, Aaron, Best Man, and my sister, Kim, Maid of Honor.

June 8th, Tuesday.

Like flowers anticipate the sun and the moon longs for the night, my heart yearns to be your wife

To have you completely and hold you close to me

To take care of you when you're sick and encourage you when you're well

To enjoy the times of increase and be inspired by your faith should we have times of need

For as long as we both shall live.

June 9th, Wednesday.

I've known you for a lifetime, or so it seems.

You lifted my world from lonely sadness, bringing it to joyful gladness

You truly are the man of my dreams.

June 11th, Friday.

Sixteen days until wedded bliss and an all-night kiss

Sixteen days until I am your wife and you share, with Jesus, my one and only life

Sixteen days and I leave you no longer, and we become, as a family, stronger

Sixteen days before we say, "I Do," and I can show you every day and every moment just how much I love you.

June 12, Saturday. We met with our wedding photographer, Holly, and set up a meeting time the next week to take our primary photos instead of taking them on the actual wedding day. We agreed that we would rather spend time with family and friends than going off somewhere to take photos. Only ceremonial and family photos would be taken that day, and portable cameras on each table for people to take candid shots of the day for us.

Next, we were off to my friend Stephanie's to drop off the items that she needed to build our centerpieces. Evan had written a poem about God being a potter and how He crafted a special pot to place a beautiful flower into. So our centerpieces were simple—a small white pot with a single Gerbera daisy planted inside. Later, we had dinner with Ashley, and we went to Calvary Chapel for Saturday Night Life. Evan wrote a note to me at some point during the service:

"It pleases the Lord to put our lives together and to take two different musical instruments to create a symphony of music, playing the same note and beating to the same count."

So that night, I went home and wrote this:

A love affair unlike any other, orchestrated by the hand of the Father

Two different instruments joined together, a symphony of music playing the same notes, beating to the same count.

Beautiful

Timeless

Perfect

June 16, Wednesday. Worked a half day, then met Evan at his house. We had appointments with Jennifer, our hairdresser and matchmaker extraordinaire, for a test run on my wedding hair and to get me ready for our wedding photoshoot, which was taking place in a few hours. My hair was perfect, and we headed over to Rose's for my dress fitting, which was also perfect, and then it was time to meet Holly at Prospect Park to take our staged photos. Evan was much more comfortable in front of the camera. I'm a realist, so staging romance was just weird to me. Holly was patient, and she really helped me to relax. We had a lot of fun. Thankfully, I had worn comfortable shoes!

June 17, Thursday. After work, I went over to Chuck and Melanie's for dinner and to create a playlist for the wedding. In 2004, I didn't own a computer, but Melanie had an Apple laptop, and together we figured out how to use iTunes to download my CDs and burn a new one from my playlist. Smartphones had not been invented yet, and I never had extra funds to purchase such a luxurious item anyway. In fact, when I arrived in California in 1985, I had never even seen a computer in real life, only in pictures, and when I started my second job since moving, I had to learn how to use one in order to do my job.

I made numerous mistakes at first, crashing the poor computer and calling the boss over the intercom, "David, there's something wrong with the computer." David was a very patient man, and after about the fortieth time, he finally explained to me that the computer was fine, the operator was the problem. As with everything else in my life, I had no patience for a slow-moving computer, and I just overwhelmed the thing.

I still laugh about it, and I still, on occasion, move too fast for even the newest models. It was slow going, downloading the songs and trying to get the playlist just right. I knew the song that I wanted us to do our first dance to; it was from the little romantic comedy that Evan and I had watched at my place a few weeks earlier. In the middle of the movie, the couple goes dancing, and the song, "Now it Can Be Told," is playing in the background. I am a huge Tony Bennett fan, and the words to this song were PERFECT for us.

Next would be a succession of Frank Sinatra, Dean Martin, and more Tony Bennett tunes. "Night and Day," "The Best is Yet to Come," "Love and Marriage," "Strangers in the Night," "What is This Thing Called Love," "Oh, What It Seemed to Be," "Memories are Made of This," "Just in Time," "Return to Me," "On the Street Where You Live," " It Had to Be You," "The Shadow of Your Smile," "Because of You." Throw in a little Harry Connick Jr. "I Could Write a Book," "Our Love is Here to Stay," and even a few contemporary songs, "What if I Loved You," "Could Not Ask for More," and "I'll Be."

Unfortunately, I haven't been able to locate an actual copy of the playlist or remember all of the songs. I guess it's true about getting older and losing your memory, but with the new digital age we live in; it is pretty easy to just make a new playlist and add some new songs that we have discovered along the way.

June 19, Saturday. I received this letter from Evan:

My Dear Adda,

I awoke this morning at 4:30 am, not with work on my mind, not with family issues invading my thoughts, and believe it or not, I wasn't even going through the wedding checklists. I awoke calmly to beautiful thoughts of you. My spiritual eyes were locked on your beautiful brown eyes and how familiar they are to my soul.

My heart leaped with love as I saw your love for Christ and now your overwhelming love for me. To be loved with this kind of love has been my deepest desire all my life. The kind of love that accepts me right where I am at, to be goofy or serious, to be wise or act like a fool, in the fullness of Christ's joy or heavy with this world's burdens, with lips that encourage or a tongue not tamed, in physical wellness or aches of sorrow, to be right or wrong, walking tall with confidence or slumped into thoughts of failure, both feet on the ground or one in my mouth, connected to the head or can't get out of bed, express my love for you or off in busy thoughts of all kinds. Your love, like mine, steps above all of this to see over them, like standing on a chair to see over the crowd and connect eyes across the room. Rising high in the sky where the eagles soar, not to look down in condemnation but to get a heavenly perspective on all matters. Yes, this is pure love, not tainted with lust or fear, doubt, or insecurities. Jesus laid down His life to express his love, and likewise, you do that for me.

To be two individuals loving this way and then to be joined together at the feet of Jesus is priceless. Honoring the Father, giving Him glory, remembering the price that He paid, and loving our Lord with great intensity. No future could be more secure than ours with Christ, with each other, and with those who will be put into our path. Our road leads to an eternity that will be spent with Jesus, our Lord and Savior, but for now, we get small glimpses of what Heaven will be like, holding you in my arms, walking hand in hand, harmonizing songs of worship and praise, and kissing the face of my beautiful one.

I am in awe to think I will share it all with you, the wonderfully favored woman of God who has accepted me above all others and now gives to me a love that comes from Heaven, bound in the pierced hands of Jesus Christ.

I love you, Adda Christine Agnew

June 21, Monday. I wrote this for Evan:

Our love exists beyond words or deeds

It is not dependent upon circumstance

It is not like the crashing waves of the sea or the state of this ugly world around us

It is like the love of Christ

Constant

Surpassing understanding

Sacrificial

Beautiful

June 25, Friday. I had taken the day off from work to get a few last-minute things done and get ready for the family gathering that evening at Evan's. For the wedding tables, along with the centerpieces, we placed compact cameras and several framed photos of us that Holly had taken at the park. She also took two of the photos and had them framed with room for people to write their best wishes on. I had never seen something like this. We still have the frames with us and cherish them. As family, and some close friends, began to arrive, Evan started up the grill. We turned on the music, and soon there was excitement in the air. My mom arrived with her boyfriend, Art, and my little sister, Tiffany. Mom looked a little angry. As someone who always tried very hard not to make Mom angry, I wondered who or what had caused this. She told me that Art had worn a printed t-shirt with what she felt was very inappropriate for the occasion, and he had refused to put on something else. He also insisted on bringing his Budweiser and, after introductions, parked himself on the back patio to smoke and enjoy his beer. Evan and I thought the whole thing was hysterical, and Aaron said that he really enjoyed talking to Art.

Art and Mom had met at the American Legion Post 106, where Mom worked and Art frequented, in the early 90s. All of Mom's daughters loved Art. He allowed our mom to truly be herself and do the things that she wanted to do. All of the other men in her life had either tried to control her or just take the fun party person out of her. Art told her that he fell in love with who she was and didn't want her to change. See why we all approved of him?

Tiffany really seemed to like Evan, and she asked him what he thought of my cat, Millie, also known as Poo Poo Kitty. When he told her that Millie had allowed him to give her a pet, Tiffany decided that we were meant to be together because Poo Poo Kitty never let anyone pet her except for me. I had "adopted" a little kitten that I found starving outside of my workplace. At first, we just called her Video Store Cat, but I decided to call her Millie. She remained at the video store, entering and exiting as she pleased, until one night, she accidentally got locked into the store after we all left and made poo-poo on the floor.

The next morning David told me that Millie needed a home, not a video store. She was my faithful companion for over seventeen years. She DID like Evan, except for the morning that he got out of bed early to do some office work, and she followed him out, probably thinking that he would feed her. Instead, he closed the office door behind him. Poo Poo Kitty came back to the bed, peed on Evan's pillow, and came over to cuddle with me. Evan came back to bed after he did his office work only to lay his head on a soiled pillow. He was pretty mad. We weren't able to get the urine smell out of the pillow and were never able to find another one like it. The pillow was a special chiropractic pillow that he had purchased years before. Evan never forgot about it.

The party was really great, and we all got better acquainted. I drove home excited, thinking that I only had two more nights to spend alone. I would be Mrs. Dahlke in about thirty hours.

June 26, Saturday. Spent the morning at Mom's visiting with my Sister Kim, her daughter Jennifer, my Niece Priscilla, and Tiff. Evan was playing golf with his brother and would be picking up the centerpieces from Steph's house, which gave me more time to relax with my family. There were so many things to do to set up for the big day, but here I was, able to spend quality time with my family because Evan was taking care of pretty much everything. As soon as I started to get frustrated with things not coming together the way I wanted them to, Evan gently told me to take care of getting my dress and ordering the invitations, and he would take care of everything else. He always likes to say, "Don't worry about the mule; just load the cart."

Later we gathered at Crabby Bob's with Evan's family for dinner with lots of talking, siblings exchanging insults, and the "kids," Ashley, Nolan, Ethan, and Kyle, entertaining us with their goofiness. As I drove home, all I could think about was that I would be Mrs. Dahlke *TOMORROW!*

Our Wedding Day

A Happening in Sylvan Park

June 27th, Sunday. I woke up early and got dressed for church. Yes, I DID go to church on my wedding day. I didn't have to be at Jennifer's until 11:30, so why not? It ended up being one of the most joyful times of worship I had ever experienced. All of the events and excitement came pouring out of me in song to "The One from whom every good and perfect gift comes." Some thought I was nuts, others understood completely.

When service was over, I texted Evan to see how things were going. I went by Mom's to pick up Kim and head over to Jenn's salon. Ashley was already there and presently having her hair styled. While we waited, Evan stopped by to bring us lunch from our caterer's La Pasta Italia, delicious sandwiches and pasta salad. We were so thankful for Evan's kindness to us. Since the ceremony didn't start until 2:00, we would have been starving by the time we were pronounced husband and wife.

After Kim and I had our hair styled, we headed over to Evan's to get dressed. I was so thankful for the help of Kim and Ashley getting me ready. Soon, Chuck and Melanie arrived to take us to the venue. Even though it was late June in southern California, the weather was perfect, not too hot, and a nice little breeze keeping everyone cool.

We arrived a bit early. Chuck turned off the truck. I guess he didn't hear me asking to keep it running so that I wouldn't melt, but soon, everyone was out of the truck, so I made my way out, and Uncle Bill came over to "give me away."

Since we were early, Evan was clamoring to get his

boutonniere on and find his bell to ring. He had one engraved with our names and wedding date. I always have it displayed, with one of our wedding photos, in our home. I began to walk down the path toward the gazebo, and there were so many bells ringing. It was a beautiful sound.

We stood together, facing Pastor Dane, who welcomed everyone to this joyous occasion, explaining his participation in the ceremony. I couldn't get married without Pastor Dane being involved. He has been my pastor for almost forty years now. It's crazy to think about it now. I was only twenty years old when I showed up at the First Baptist Church of Colton, CA. However, I had moved to Oasis about four years earlier because Chuck wanted to play saxophone on the worship team, and they started going there. I missed being at church with them, so I moved over a few months later. Because of this move and his familiarity with Evan, Pastor Steve Mason performed the vows and declaration part of the ceremony.

Our Wedding Vows

"I, Adda, take you, Evan, to be my lawfully wedded husband. To have and to hold from this day forward, to love and to cherish, in sickness and in health, in good times and bad times for as long as we both shall live."

Neither of us wanted to write our own vows, too much pressure, so we decided that we would use these simple traditional vows on our wedding day. Before we said "I DO," though, we actually took time to think about each one of the vows, their true meaning, and what our promise to each other and to God was actually going to look like, in a literal sense.

For me, they went something like this: "I, Adda, accept you, Evan, as my choice of husband. I will keep you and hold you from this day until one of us passes away. I will *cherish* you, for you are the most important person in my life."

"I will love you in all of the forms of love that we have learned about. (Eros-romantic love. Eros is an intense sexual desire for someone that is passionate and can be overwhelming. This is the origin of the word erotic.) "I will love you sexually and give myself to you. I will not look to other people or things in order to be sexually satisfied. I will be faithful to you and will not withhold sex from you."

(*Phileo,* meaning close and devoted friendship. In Romans 12:10, Paul tells us to be devoted to one another in love. The Greek word that he used was phileo.). *"I promise you that I will love you as my best and closest friend. I will share my feelings with you, spend time with you, and go on adventures and have fun with you."*

(In the Hebrew language, *hesed* is another word for love and is used to describe God's steadfast, undying love for us. Hesed is a love in action. Doing nice things, being loyal and kind, going above and beyond.) *"I promise to hesed you, love you actively, put you first in all things, be nice when I speak to you, and treat you in a loving manner."*

(*Agape* love is my favorite, for it is the purest of all. It means to love unconditionally, whether or not the other person loves you back. For a biblical reference, we look to First Corinthians Chapter 13:4-8 for a perfect description of this form of love: Love is patient, love is kind. It does not envy, it does not boast, it is not proud. It is not rude. It is not self-seeking, it is not easily angered, it keeps no record of wrongs. Love does not delight in evil but rejoices with the truth.) *"I promise to agape you, to love you even when you're being a pain. I will be patient with you even when we disagree and can't come to a compromise quickly. I will be kind to you and happy when you are successful, even if I'm not so successful at the time. I will not be arrogant when I am right, nor will I put my needs before yours. I will do my best to always make you look good and to keep my cool even when you make me furious. I will not keep a list of your faults and failures, but I will forgive you as God has forgiven me. I will not agree with the evil practices of others or what culture says is acceptable. I will do my best to keep your reputation intact, and I will trust you to lead our home in a godly manner. I will remain hopeful and will keep going even when I'm tired and want to give up."*

"I will do whatever I can to help you to be healthy and strong, and should you get sick, I will take care of you and supply whatever you need in order to get well. When times are good, I will celebrate them with you. Should we happen upon bad times, I will be faithful and loyal to you, and I will never give up on you."

We're on year twenty, and I hope that Evan still feels loved, cherished, supported, and respected. It has been my greatest mission to be a good wife for him. He really deserves it.

After the declaration and announcement, Evan's current pastor, Rick, asked people to gather around us, and he prayed that God would use us mightily and for marital happiness and success. Evan's mom, Janice, sang a prophetic song for us, and then it was SUPPOSED to be time for our first dance. However, because everyone else had arrived much earlier, no one had gotten to say hi to me or give me hugs before the ceremony. Now, EVERYONE wanted to hug and talk. Evan came to get me for the dance, but I wasn't able to break free for a few more minutes. He liked telling people that I was disobedient just thirty seconds after becoming his wife. HA-HA.

We did our dance to "Now It Can Be Told" and then invited everyone to come up and dance. After a few songs, we headed out to do the table greetings. My feet were killing me, and I ended up taking the unholy shoes off. No one would have ever known had I worn my boots. The dress was long enough, and I could have pulled it off, but NO, I had to get proper wedding shoes. Saying hello to everyone was wonderful, but it took a LONG time because we had well over 350 people there.

People were taking lots of photos with disposable cameras, and one of my friends, Debra, had made some beautiful bookmarks for everyone to take home. They had a picture of us at the top and then two poems, one written by me and one by Evan. Instead of a traditional wedding cake, we decided to have Hawaiian Shaved Ice. I had to be careful not to spill grape "stuff" on my dress since I very often have issues with such things.

We took a few minutes for Holly to take a family photo for us, as well as a photo of the Gang. (We lost Mike some years later. And then there were five.)

Our Bookmarks

When you hold me close, I feel the Father's love

So warm and safe, satisfying the deepest longing for His touch

When you kiss me, I feel like the Bride of Christ

That passion that led Him to die, compelling Him onto that Cross

When you look into my eyes, I see a mighty Warrior,

Who sweeps me off of my feet

We rise up together to conquer all of the enemies of Christ!

When you say my name, it is as though I am hearing music that exceeds the beauty of Beethoven

When you leave, my heart leaves with you, for it is yours and cannot be separated from you.

When I see you again, it comes back to me

Filled with more joy and adoration than before.

And when you pray for me, I feel Heaven moving

To honor your every request

Adda, June 2004

Masterpiece

My Lord is a gardener, a gardener indeed
He's planted a flower from a little seed
He chose a special soil for the flower to grow
Watering it daily, the water of life does flow
The flower soon grew upright in bloom
What a precious flower my Lord did groom

The Lord is a potter, a potter of clay
He's been at work on a pot this very day
Shaping and molding preparing a great pot
For a special flower, my Lord has brought

My Lord is an artist, and He's done a lot
Knowing which flower is for which pot
Nothing is more beautiful than the work of His hands
You can see how much, across these lands
They were crafted alone and now have become
Not two of God's works, but ONE

So when you see this work of art
Always remember that the Lord is part
Blessed is the flower, for the pot is strong
Protected and held up all the days long
The pot has a treasure, a treasure to call mine
It's a beautiful flower, so precious and kind

Evan 1995 (Written for his brother Aaron's wedding but
perfectly fit ours, too)

It was time to say our goodbyes and head out to the beach and The Beachcomber Inn. We decided to postpone taking a honeymoon trip until the next month, so we were only going to the beach for a few days. The Beachcomber is located in San Clemente, right on the beach. I had come to love the sound of the ocean and the cool breezes, so this was the perfect place to spend our first nights as husband and wife. Someone had made a sign that said, "Evan and Adda's Wedding," so we grabbed the sign and headed for the truck. The last thing that I did was hand my friend Bonnie my bouquet, a special gift for her with hopes and prayers for a beautiful wedding of her own.

If there was traffic to the beach, we didn't notice, nor did we care. We were married now and certain that God would do great things for and through us as a couple. Before check-in, the owners of the Beachcomber came out to take our "Just Married" photo and showed us the room. Believe it or not, we took a little time to enjoy the view before anything of a private nature began.

<u>Mini-Moon</u>

Somewhere on a Beach

June 28th, Monday. This was the BEST Monday EVER, as I woke up next to my husband, having spent the best day and night with him. We had our coffee out on the patio, overlooking the Pacific Ocean, and we talked about the beauty of God's creation and our thankfulness for having been thrown together in the whirlwind that was our romance.

We had a huge number of wedding cards to go through, but first, we had breakfast as we were hungry, having not eaten in almost twenty-four hours. There was a small cafe just down the street, so we got ready and walked there. It was a magnificent day and the cafe was busy with fellow travelers. We both ordered oatmeal with sides of bacon and fruit.

Evan was being kind, not ordering eggs, for he knew that I loathed them. (Strangely enough, when I was a little girl, I LOVED eggs and wanted to eat them every day. I would drive my mom crazy asking for them at practically every meal, and to top it off, I only ate them over easy without bread of any kind, which would just make her gag. I can't be sure of the time frame, but at some point, I started hating eggs, and to this day, I cannot stand to smell an egg cooking or see one on a plate.)

Back to breakfast. When our food arrived, I doctored my oatmeal with only the brown sugar, but Evan had the brown sugar as well as ALL of the other fixings that were offered. *Yuck,* I thought, which isn't surprising if you know me and all of my peculiarities when it comes to food. (I hate when different foods touch each other on the plate, and I NEVER have gravy of any kind, nor do I mix my foods, like mashed potatoes and corn. YUCK!)

What was really interesting about this oatmeal was how creamy it was. I wasn't used to it coming out this way, so I asked the waitress how it was prepared. Besides the usual water-to-oatmeal ratio, they also used a good deal of half and half while it was cooking.

Well, I fell in love, and I had never wanted to eat oatmeal again without the added half and half. Not a very good diet practice, for sure, so I don't eat oatmeal very often anymore.

After breakfast, we went back to the hotel to relax and open some of the wedding cards. We were overwhelmed with the generosity and love poured out upon us. We have certainly been blessed with amazing friends, family, and co-workers. With over three hundred and fifty guests, it was going to take quite a while to get through all of the cards, so we decided to take a break and go do some sightseeing.

I had never been to this particular beach, so we drove around the city and marveled at the number of people on the beach. As we drove toward a Volkswagen dealership, Evan said to me, "You know, you have always wanted to check out the new Beetles. We should take one for a test drive." Now, at that time, I didn't know Evan all that well. I had only met him in March, so I didn't know that when he said, "You know," and it pertained to a particular vehicle; it meant that we would end up purchasing said vehicle that very day.

We found a cute lemon drop Beetle, certified pre-owned, and it was immaculate with low miles. I have to admit, I really loved it and wanted it; however, I had just purchased a brand-new vehicle and didn't think this was a necessary purchase.

Evan told the salesman to make an offer that we couldn't refuse, and he did. So I purchased a little yellow beetle while on my honeymoon, and we drove home the next morning in separate vehicles.

This would not be the last time that I would hear my husband say, "You know…" followed by a statement about some other vehicle that we would purchase that same day. Evan DID tell me several times during our long courtship that it would be dangerous to be married to him. Over the years, I have come to understand his meaning in many different ways.

<u>Our Honeymoon</u>

The Great Escape

It all started with a movie, "The Majestic," a favorite of mine yet never seen by Evan until we met. In the movie, Jim Carey plays a Hollywood screenwriter who has been named a communist sympathizer by someone else in the industry. (Congressional accusations of communist influence in the film industry began in 1941. A blacklist involved the practice of denying employment to entertainment industry professionals believed to be or to have been Communists or sympathizers. Actors, screenwriters, directors, musicians, and other American entertainment professionals were barred from work by the studios (reference britanicca.com).

Carey's character, Peter Appleton, leaves town to avoid facing the congressional committee and ends up on a beach after wrecking his car on a bridge. At this point, he has no memory of who he is and is found on the beach by an old man with a dog. The man takes him to his small town to get him medical help, and he is mistaken for a long-lost WWII soldier, Luke Trimble, the son of a man named Harry.

Watch the movie. It's GREAT! The beautiful cinematography and location shooting really intrigued me, and I wanted to go to all of the places that were featured in the movie. There are lighthouses, beaches, and a gorgeous Victorian home-filled town with an amazing hillside cemetery. Yes, I wanted to go to these places, and that is what we did on our Great Escape.

August 2nd, Monday. We flew from Ontario, CA, to Oakland, CA, early in the morning, too early for me at least, and upon arrival, headed over to the car rental place. We had reserved a small compact since it was only the two of us, and we packed light. Evan looked around at the other vehicles, admiring a cute Ford Escape and saying how fun it would be to have that for the trip. Well, as happens to him often, he was told that they ran out of compacts and that we were getting a free upgrade, the very Ford Escape that he had mentioned.

Soon, we were on our way to see some beautiful landscapes and several lighthouses along State Route 1, a highway that runs along the Pacific coastline of California. I was already a bit shaky from the plane ride, so the winding roads of HWY 1 were making me completely dizzy, and I had to lie down. Here we were, in the most beautiful place on earth, and I was lying down, and Evan was playing tour guide describing all the different colors and landscapes.

With the Pacific Ocean on our left and gigantic Redwoods on our right, this truly was a paradise. Evan would stop in the middle of the road to take photos on our little Olympus Digital (no iPhone existed at that time), and then he would show them to me. For some reason, there was just no one else on the road. It was as if God had cleared all traffic so that we, or should I say, Evan, could enjoy the drive. He drove slowly and gently so as not to make me sicker.

Late afternoon, we arrived at our first destination—The Point Arena Lighthouse. This was NOT the lighthouse that was featured in The Majestic, but it WAS from a movie, another favorite of mine, "Forever Young" (1992, Romantic Fantasy), starring Mel Gibson. The lighthouse and its surrounding structures were featured in the grand finale of the movie, where Mel's character is reunited with the love of his former life, a woman that he mistakenly believed had been killed in a traffic accident.

The beautiful Cape Cod-style home was there, with the

enormous lighthouse just beyond. We checked in and then strolled through the grounds, all the while enjoying the Pacific Ocean's view and cool breezes. We took a few pictures and headed into town for dinner. The small town of Point Arena is pretty quiet, with a few taverns, art galleries, and eateries. However, the real beauty lies in the serene walking trails, fishing, and beach combing.

Dinner was a surprise. The Arena Bar and Grill looked simple on the outside, but inside, it was just as nice and fancy as a big city restaurant would be, and the food was amazing, too! Evan and I are both food lovers, in general, and many of our trips have been designed with food in mind.

This was our first real outing together, so it was fun getting to know each other in new ways and just having time to "BE" and exist together. We drove back to the lighthouse and fell asleep in the warmth of the fireplace, listening to the crashing ocean waves.

August 3rd, Tuesday. We took a tour of the grounds and lighthouse with the temporary lighthouse keeper. We talked to her as she told us of her own history with the lighthouse, and we told her a little about our whirlwind engagement and wedding.

When it was time to climb up the 141 stairs to the top of the lighthouse, I was a bit weary. As I made my way up the winding staircase, I had to stop and catch my breath as well as avoid looking down from the height. Vertigo was never far away, so I had to be careful not to make any sudden moves, either. When we got to the top, the view was so incredible that you could see for miles out to sea. Looking into the special cut glass of the lens made me dizzy, and then having to go back down all of those stairs wasn't great. Evan took his time and helped me to reach the bottom safely. He always takes good care of me.

We had planned to stay for two nights but decided to head to our next destination, Point Cabrillo, earlier. As we drove away, we talked about what it would be like to live a quiet, simple life as lighthouse keepers in a beautiful, remote place such as this one. I would welcome the quiet and peaceful existence while reading and writing, taking long walks, and listening to the sound of the ocean all day and night. Evan, however, would be bored out of his mind in just a few weeks with no interaction with people or something else to keep him busy.

Highway 1 took us all the way up the coast. First, it took us to Mendocino, where we stopped for lunch and greatly admired the town with breathtaking views and old Victorian-style homes. We ate at the Bayview Restaurant, and it was fabulous. Everything was fresh and delicious. Evan had a crab cake sandwich, a Po' Boy, you could say, and I had BBQ salmon.

With our tummies happy, we drove the short distance to Point Cabrillo, the lighthouse from The Majestic movie. The walk to the lighthouse was about a half mile and certainly an important part of the experience. There was a new home being built along the path, as well as two older, already-established homes. One of which was featured in the movie as the home of the town doctor and his daughter, the love interest of Jim Carey's character.

As we approached the lighthouse, I recapped the scene where the two lovers run to the lighthouse and climb to the top of the tower for their first kiss. We had a kiss of our own at this newly renovated and beautiful piece of history. I had taken three motion sickness preventers before leaving that morning, so I looked a bit under the influence in the few pictures that we took.

Back in the car, we made our way up to Fort Bragg, an adorable and quite expensive little place with great old-town charm and shops to match. I wanted some mint chip ice cream, and we went into two places without any luck. We asked a townie where we could get some specialty ice cream. Is mint chip a specialty ice cream? We were directed to the Cowlick Ice Cream Shop, where I got my mint chip and Evan got to try something new—root beer float ice cream.

With both of us happy, we made our way to HWY 101 for the next part of our trip, stopping along the way to view the awe-inspiring giant redwood trees in an area called "The Avenue of the Giants." The Redwood Highway was a very narrow two-lane road with many winding turns.

We looked and felt so small compared to the giant redwoods!

I was pretty sick by the time we got to the 101, but after a while, I was able to sit up straight and enjoy the rest of the drive. We decided to head to Eureka, CA, and spend the night in one of their Victorian bed-and-breakfasts. With all of the more prominent bed-and-breakfasts in Eureka already occupied, we drove around town for a while and happened upon "The Old Town Inn," a small Victorian home with beautiful blue hydrangeas and an all-important vacancy with a private bath.

The rooms were small, and the furnishings were old, but we both thought it had a certain charm in its simplicity. After checking in, we headed back downtown for dinner, finding an amazing sushi restaurant called "The Ritz," and then to a quaint little coffee shop for a slice of chocolate-swirled cheesecake. Back in our room, we were exhausted from the eventful day and fell asleep watching Hope Floats.

August 4th, Wednesday. Before marriage, my mornings were short and rushed in order to get ready for work and be there on time, never needing to have or provide conversation. Now, I was waking up next to a man who loves mornings and is always ready for meaningful conversation during our coffee time.

This particular morning, we decided to bathe in the giant claw foot tub while enjoying our coffee, taking our time and making our way downstairs to breakfast much later than the other guests, but we were still able to meet them and talk for a while.

Today, we drove to Ferndale, CA, where much of "The Majestic" was filmed. Big Victorian homes lined the streets, and even the downtown was like going back in time. Lovely shops and happy people were all around us, and we both fell in love with this little town. In fact, we talked at length about looking into purchasing a Victorian bed-and-breakfast of our own. How fun it would be to meet and bless people from all over the country. Evan loves to restore and maintain and I love to cook and decorate. It was a subject that we went back to time and again.

My favorite part of town was the old hillside cemetery with tombstones dating back to the 1800's. We probably spent an hour just walking around and reading the heartfelt remembrances of loved ones for the ones that they had lost.

Even after driving through the entire town and stopping in some shops, we were still several hours from check-in time, so we headed back to Eureka to watch a movie, "The Bourne Supremacy," the second in the Bourne series, at the Broadway Theater. We shared a Sprite and buttered popcorn, taking care not to eat too much so as to have room for dinner at Curley's Bar and Grill in Downtown Ferndale, a highly recommended eatery housed in an old Victorian hotel.

The movie was great, and we were anxious to get back to Ferndale to check into The Shaw House Inn, where we would stay for only one lovely night. Upon arrival, we met Paula, the owner of the inn and a very delightful woman. She explained that the inn was built in 1854 as a labor of love for a cherished fiancée and is the oldest structure in Ferndale and the oldest bed-and-breakfast in California. It is surrounded by a one-acre park filled with hundred-year-old redwoods and rhododendrons. She gave us a tour of the house and then showed us to our room.

Tears filled my eyes as I took in the beauty of the room, complete with a claw foot tub at the end of the bed. (Since then, I have always wanted to have a claw foot tub in my own bedroom, but Evan never saw the sense or resale value of the idea.) We took our showers and got ready for dinner at Curley's. Walking into town on this perfect evening was definitely my favorite part of the trip thus far.

We got to Curley's and informed the hostess that we were on our honeymoon and asked if they had any secluded spots for us to dine. She led us to a little corner with a small table for two and a window to look out to the downtown area. We asked our waiter to go outside and snap a photo of us.

The music was a mix of classics from the forties and fifties, and I shared with Evan that I had dreamed of being a jazz lounge singer when I was younger. He said that had to be why I knew so many songs, most of which he had never heard in his life. Of course, my parents were music lovers, and I grew up listening to a wide variety of styles and artists. My favorite was Frank Sinatra, mostly due to the fact that Ol' Blue Eyes was Mom's favorite singer, and I wanted to do and love everything that she did.

Dinner was fabulous, and we were definitely finding out that the other person was a foodie of sorts. Evan being the adventurous one who would try just about anything, while I delight in sampling the classics prepared in various styles. Not having frequented many fancy restaurants in the past, I also discovered Creme Brûlée, a custard dish with torched sugar topping. We would both later develop a rather unhealthy and budget-unfriendly love for fine dining and continue the trend, even now.

We walked hand in hand back to our room, where we enjoyed a bubble bath while reading through our book, "The Five Love Languages." Evan's love language was "words of affirmation," and mine was "physical touch." We were learning how to love each other in a more practical way and preparing, although we didn't know it then, for a ministry that God would call us to in the future.

August 5th, Thursday. The inn had a full house of guests, and as we all gathered at the large dining table, introductions and lots of conversation ensued. Breakfast was as expected, fancy and delicious. We said our goodbyes, packed, and got on the road. I was sad to leave this wonderful little town and made a plan, in my mind, to return for an anniversary trip in the future. It was close to a five-hour drive back to San Francisco, and we passed some beautiful wine country along the way.

Back in town, we parked the car and walked down to Pier 39, now a familiar place since the engagement trip. I wanted to go back to Bubba Gump's and have the same Shrimpin' Dippin' meal that I had the last time while Evan had shrimp pasta. He was a good sport since shrimp really isn't his thing.

We discussed some possibilities for the last night of our Great Escape, deciding to pick up a newspaper from the corner newsstand, and, seeing that we were too early for most performing arts, we looked at some local clubs to see if there was anything interesting happening. We found a listing for The Plush Room, a cabaret lounge located in The York Hotel in the Lower Nob Hill District, with singer Julie Budd headlining that week. Funny, we thought, we were just talking about my wanting to be a lounge singer, and here was an opportunity to see a live cabaret show. I was excited, as this was my kind of music, and Evan just enjoyed watching me being excited.

The floor was covered with tables of various sizes and couples of various nationalities and orientations. We changed clothes in the very fancy restrooms, and I couldn't wait for the show to begin. Our waiter informed us of the two-drink minimum, so we asked for a list of their non-alcoholic beverages. We settled on San Pellegrino Limonata. We laughed at his overly dramatic pronunciation, "LimoNATA," and thoroughly enjoyed people watching as the club filled up.

Next, Julie Budd was introduced, and for the next hundred or so minutes, we were delightfully entertained. I knew every song, and Evan enjoyed the fact that I knew every song.

After the show, we drove to Oakland, where we would stay at the Motel Six Oakland Airport Motel. We laugh about it now, but after staying in these luxurious bed-and-breakfasts, to have this be the last night of our honeymoon, was pretty sorry.

Neither of us had thought about it, and upon entering our room and having it smell like smoke and be old and dingy left Evan feeling shame for not planning ahead on this one. I was tired and wanted to just get into bed and sleep, but Evan hates the smell of smoke, so he complained to the night manager that the room smelled of smoke. He gave us a different room, which, lo and behold, smelled of smoke.

You see, just because the motel was now smoke-free didn't mean that they painted the rooms, changed out the carpets and drapes, or even the bed linens. Everything still smelled of smoke, and it would be true of the next room if we had decided to complain some more. It was much too late to try to find another place to stay, so we resigned to stay and make the best of it. Sleep came quickly.

August 6th, Friday. Woke up feeling rested, despite our drab surroundings, and got ready for our flight home. The flight was delayed, so we passed the time people watching and reminiscing about the trip. Evan's favorite part was seeing the amazing landscapes and the food. My favorite part was visiting some of the places that I had seen in my favorite movies (there would be more opportunities for these types of road trips in our future. More on those later).

We were informed that our gate number had changed, so we rushed to get to our plane, Evan taking care of the luggage and me trying to keep up. On the plane, Evan had a short nap while I read my battered copy of "Walden."

Outside the terminal, Ashley and Janice awaited our arrival with smiles. We enjoyed a wonderful lunch at Benihana, and then we were off to Ashley's dance rehearsal and to pick up her dress for the show the following day, then a visit with Mom and Tiff at Mom's place.

Another wonderful day in the life of Mrs. Adda Christine Dahlke.

Part Two

Great Expectations

And They Lived...
Happily Ever After

When you can count, on one hand, the number of real boyfriends you have had by the time you're in your mid-thirties and you haven't been involved with anyone in over a decade, a person might get swept up into a sort of La La Land of the romantic fantasy kind. I wasn't interested in stories of beautiful people misbehaving or men mistreating women and getting away with it just because they were rich or dangerous. I pined for a nice guy that I could be attracted to. I knew a few nice guys, but there wasn't any spark or interest beyond friendship.

So I lived, vicariously for a time, through my favorite movies or books that depicted romance in cute, funny, and friendly ways above sordid or crude ones. Saturday mornings were spent either watching a favorite movie, probably seen more than a dozen times before, or reading a good Jane Austen tale of unrequited love between those of different social classes. These stories almost always begin with the couple in question hating each other for various reasons, most of them being good ones, and they aren't, generally speaking, very realistic. Isn't that the point, though?

I'm a bit of a marriage behaviorist, so I love to take these fictional couples and flesh out their characters to decide whether they were really made for each other or if they could even have a successful relationship.

Perhaps some of my favorite couples are yours as well. Perhaps your expectations of relationships are vastly different than mine, or you see things in a less cynical or more idyllic sort of way. Maybe you don't even like romantic stories and would rather have a root canal than watch or read about couples in love. Maybe you have never read a Jane Austen or E.M. Forester novel or any other novel for that matter. If so, you might want to skip this entire section.

Couple Number One: C.K. Dexter Haven and Tracy Lord (The Philadelphia Story, 1940)

When the movie begins, the couple is at the obvious end of their relationship; his bags are packed, and she is hurling the rest of his belongings out the door, including his golf clubs, one of which she happily breaks over her knee. His anger propels him to strike her, but he decides to merely shove her, and she lands on the floor holding her neck. It DOES get better, I promise.

The next scene opens with Tracy and her family preparing for her wedding, which will take place in a few days, where she will say "I Do" to George, a man enamored by her beauty and place in society. George is also a man who will be easily put in his place and agreeable to any of Tracy's decision-making. What George lacks is backbone, passion, and social stature. Tracy would be marrying down, so to speak, as George would be considered below her in socioeconomic class. So why is Tracy planning to marry this man? Because her first husband, C.K. Dexter Haven, was her equal, and they didn't get along well because of it.

Rich, handsome, funny, and talented, Dexter would be a good match for just about any woman. He was also a man that Tracy couldn't boss around and who saw through her pretentiousness. They fought hard and often, I'm sure. Their divorce was probably as ugly as their marriage was, and yet, when Dexter arrives back on the scene, Tracy's family welcomes him with open arms. This gives the impression that they believe the problems in the Haven marriage were more Tracy's rather than Dexter's fault.

There are other subplots that are adorable, especially Jimmy Stewart's character, Mike, who is a serious book author but is being humbled greatly by his current employer, Spy Magazine. Mike and Tracy become attracted to each other, mostly due to the partaking of alcohol. Stewart's drunken scenes are hilarious, especially when he ends up at the home of Dexter, whom he always refers to as "C.K. Dexter Haven." I'm laughing right now as I can hear his drawl! "Oh, C.K Dexter Haven." If you have yet to see this gem of a movie, I'm sure that it is streaming somewhere. It's hard to generalize it as there are just so many wonderful scenes.

Back to Dexter and Tracy. Through a series of conversations and mishaps, Tracy ends up calling off her wedding to George; however, all of the guests are already in the chapel, and Tracy must now fess up to her most current debacle. Mike decides to ask Tracy to marry him just to save face, but she appreciatively declines. Now Dexter steps up and proposes to her, and the two walk down the aisle imagining that this second chance at love will be successful and that they will live "Happily Ever After."

As much as I like this ending (I like most happy endings but not all of them), I wonder about their chances for success. Pride and arrogance don't disappear in an instant, not to mention grudge-holding and unforgiveness. Dexter seems to have grown in character in the two-year separation; he has quit drinking, a major problem in their first marriage, and has become more introspective. Tracy, on the other hand, has been humbled by just about every person in the story, but can it last? Has she become a new person overnight? She promises to be "more yare," a nautical term used several times in the story to refer to an easy-going, swift, and well-maintained ship or vessel. They will have none of the conventional problems with life, such as money or position. Their children will be beautiful and will grow up without having to face any hardships (much the same as their parents did), and they will look forward to the best schools and anything they could possibly need or desire.

I give Dexter and Tracy a seventy-five percent chance of happiness. Not the kind of happiness that comes from the struggle and hard work of real-life marriage, theirs would be of the most fantastical kind, the kind that this grown-up and married woman knows better than to expect, but it sure would be fun to see if it were real.

Couple Number Two: Mr. Darcy and Elizabeth Bennett (Pride and Prejudice, 1813 Novel, 1995 Mini-Series being the best film version)

Pride and Prejudice opens with Mrs. Bennett, a very annoying character, announcing to Mr. Bennett that a young man of great fortune will be occupying a nearby estate. He will need to find a suitable wife in order to enjoy his life of leisure, and since Mr. Bennett had five daughters and naught a son to inherit, the answer to all of their problems would be for at least one of those daughters to marry extremely well. Mr. Bennett is not in agreement and refuses to visit the young man upon his arrival at the estate.

When I read the book, probably in high school, the mother character was much less annoying because whilst reading a book, one decides, on their own, how each character should sound. While watching the film version, written and directed by Andrew Davies, we are bombarded with the voice of Mrs. Bennett, which causes the brain to wish for deafness. "My poor nerves!" she continually laments. "MY nerves" is what I continually think when watching any version of this classic.

Now, let's talk about the lead players, Elizabeth Bennett and Mr. Darcy. Elizabeth is one of my favorite literary characters because of her no-nonsense view of life, yet she is also a generous and kind person. She lacks the social standing that money secures because her father's estate only generates two thousand pounds in income per year. Compare that to Mr. Darcy's ten thousand pounds per year, and it gives us an idea of how wide the gap would be in social and economic terms. She doesn't suffer fools very well, especially those of the upper class who behave badly, yet she could still be vulnerable in the presence of a charming man such as Lieutenant Wickham.

Mr. Darcy, on the other hand, is the owner of a very large estate and wants for nothing. However, he does need to find a good woman with whom to produce an heir and share a happy life. His social position greatly limits his prospects, and he is heavily guarded against lesser or lower-class women's attention. I believe that Mr. Darcy is a misconceived literary character in that most people make him out to be a cold-hearted person who doesn't care at all about anyone of lower standing. I believe that he IS a kind and thoughtful man who just feels that he needs to be guarded against those who could try to take advantage of his family's estate, just like, as we learn, Lieutenant Wickham did.

Darcy and Elizabeth first meet at a ball, the social gatherings of the time. The young man occupying the nearby estate turned out to be Mr. Bingley, a man of 5,000 a year with a very agreeable disposition. He arrives at the ball with his two sisters as well as Mr. Darcy, who is seen to have a proud and disagreeable countenance by all attendees, and his first words about Elizabeth, speaking to Mr. Bingley, were that she was "tolerable, but not handsome enough to tempt me."

Elizabeth reacted by playfully telling her friends of the incident, "delighting in anything ridiculous." What an inauspicious first impression! Some would say that I am misled concerning my tenancy to give Mr. Darcy any amount of grace for his being such a proud and arrogant man. However, he is, first and foremost, a rules person, like myself. The rules are always meticulously followed, and failure is never an option. He simply MUST choose wisely as well as according to the social class structure of the time. Mr. Darcy has my sympathies, but he would never desire them.

Darcy and Elizabeth meet again at the home of Sir William Lucas, the father of Elizabeth's best friend, Charlotte Lucas. While playfully interacting with a soldier, Elizabeth notices Mr. Darcy listening in on the conversation and turns her attention to him. Darcy has been wrestling with unwanted feelings and curiosity about Elizabeth, so it makes sense that he is watching her every move and honing in on her conversations. Charlotte opens the door for more discovery by asking Elizabeth to play the piano and sing a song for all of them. Her performance is described by Mr. Darcy as "pleasing but by no means capital." High praise, indeed! The dancing begins, and Darcy is neither impressed nor engaged, but when offered the chance to dance with Elizabeth, she turns him down on the simple principle that he would never choose dancing as a form of fun or pleasure, especially under the present circumstances. Owing to misconception and in struggle to save face, Elizabeth is judgmental and quite prideful herself.

The next time our lovers meet is at Netherfield Park, the rented estate of Mr. Bingley, whose sisters had been entertaining Jane Bennett, Elizabeth's older and more beautiful sister. Jane became ill because of Mrs. Bennett's scheme to keep her there overnight by sending her on horseback in the rain instead of lending her the family carriage. Elizabeth walks to Netherfield in the rain upon hearing of her sister's illness. Mr. Darcy defends Elizabeth from Bingley's sister's ridicule of her appearance upon arriving, as well as her lack of conversation and manners at the dinner table. This is where we start to see Darcy's love for Elizabeth blossoming. He is STILL guarded concerning her, but he is slowly melting, so to speak. Through several scenes, Darcy and Elizabeth seem to understand each other and go as far as to defend the other person when attacked. It is good to mention here that Mr. Darcy is smitten; however, "he believed that if it were not for the inferiority of her connections, he should be in some danger." Ah, love…

Soon after returning home, Elizabeth meets Lieutenant Wickham, a handsome officer whose charms and good looks immediately attract Elizabeth, who has all but forgotten Mr. Darcy. Darcy and Bingley soon appear, and there is a strange, uncomfortable exchange between Darcy and Wickham. Elizabeth notices this and later inquires to know about it from Wickham. He tells her lies about Darcy, which she believes, and so, for some time, has an even greater disdain for Darcy.

Mr. Bingley gives a ball at Netherfield, and the entire Bennett household attends, as does Mr. Darcy and a quite ridiculous long-lost family member of Mr. Bennett's who has his eyes on Elizabeth as a possible wife. Elizabeth wants to spend the entire evening with Lt. Wickham yet is forced to dance with her cousin, Mr. Collins. Learning that Wickham would not make an appearance that evening catches Elizabeth off guard, and she carelessly accepts the hand of Darcy for a dance. It doesn't go well, and they part until dinner is served. Seated across the table from each other, Elizabeth is embarrassed by her mother's imprudence in announcing to her table mate that her daughter Jane would soon be engaged to their host and doing so in her usual loud manner. A disastrous evening for Elizabeth and Darcy alike, but they WOULD meet again.

Elizabeth takes a trip to visit her best friend Charlotte, who is now married to Mr. Collins, and they reside at the estate of Lady Catherine De Bourgh, a most snobbish woman, who is Darcy's Aunt and has ideas of Darcy marrying her sickly daughter, Lady Anne. They learn that Darcy is to come to visit, and Elizabeth is not excited in the least. They do share a few good exchanges thanks to Darcy's cousin, Colonel Fitzwilliam, but during Darcy's visit, she will learn, from the Colonel, of Darcy's interference with Bingley and Jane's almost attachment, advising his friend to break it off with her and find someone who is more agreeable and that he was the cause of their leaving Netherfield. She is, therefore, in no mood to receive Darcy's declaration of his love for her, which comes only hours after her conversation with Colonel Fitzwilliam. All seems lost, but Elizabeth receives a letter from Darcy explaining himself as well as clarifying his dislike of Mr. Wickham. She now feels ashamed of her prejudicial attitude and her poor judgment concerning Wickham. Her feelings for Darcy begin to change as she returns home with her Jane in tow.

Elizabeth leaves home to travel with Aunt and Uncle Gardiner, brother of Mrs. Bennett, on a tour of the country estates of Derbyshire. Pemberly was just a few miles out of their way, and her aunt desired to see it as she had grown up in the general area. Elizabeth feels distressed at the idea of possibly seeing Mr. Darcy there. They arrive to learn that Mr. Darcy will be returning the next day, so the housekeeper gives them a tour of the home, all the while complimenting her master at every turn. Later, as they are standing outside, Elizabeth is astonished to see Darcy walking toward her! She blushes, feeling ashamed at being there, thinking, "How strange it must appear to him for me to be here." Darcy is all awkward politeness, and Elizabeth cannot wait to get away from there.

He joins them again later as they tour the grounds of Pemberly. Elizabeth is still shocked by Darcy's politeness, as there is none of the disdain for her family members she had been used to. She is later introduced to Miss Darcy and reunited with Mr. Bingley. She feels none of the anger toward him as she did previously and is further astonished and a bit confused by Mr. Darcy's continued mild manner and kind countenance. After dining at Pemberly, Elizabeth tries to figure out what her feelings for Mr. Darcy actually are. As she contemplates his behavior since her angry outburst, she realizes what a wonderful man he is and falls in love with him. Her feelings are furthered, still, when a family catastrophe springs Darcy into action to help her. When it seemed that a relationship between them was now impossible, Darcy showed none of the disdain for Elizabeth's family or the silliness that was constantly evident in them. When all seems lost, Elizabeth now imagines what her life would have been like had she accepted Mr. Darcy's proposal or had she not shared her family's crisis with him.

Soon, the family crisis is averted; however, Elizabeth is unaware, at this point, that it was Mr. Darcy who saved the day, not her Uncle Gardener, as everyone believes to be the case. True love is so close.

Elizabeth learns that it was indeed Mr. Darcy who settled accounts and made sure that her family would not be further scandalized, so when Bingley returns to Netherfield, she is very curious to see how Mr. Darcy behaves toward her and her family. They dine at the Bennett's, and Jane and Bingley's romance is rekindled while Elizabeth has now concluded that Mr. Darcy's affections toward her have vanished. It is sad, at this point, to recollect that for a woman in this time period, to approach a man was unthinkable. She could only conclude that he felt nothing for her, according to his not even attempting to speak to her. So sad.

Mr. Bingley proposes to Jane, and Elizabeth is happy for her, but can you imagine, if this were real life, how you would feel? Your own hopes for love and a good marriage shattered. I guess this is another reason that I love Elizabeth. She thinks of her family's future and well-being instead of her own disappointment.

Mr. Bingley spends many hours at Longbourne from this time forward, and during this time, Elizabeth receives a personal visit from Lady Catherine DeBourg instructing her to turn down any proposals of marriage from her nephew, Mr. Darcy! What have we here? Mr. Darcy has informed his aunt that he will not marry his cousin, though his mother and aunt had wished it to be so since their infancy. Elizabeth informs Lady Catherine that she will not give her assurance that she will not accept a proposal, and Lady Catherine must return home disappointed.

Mr. Darcy returns to Netherfield, and so he and Elizabeth are reunited. Their interaction is uncomfortable until Elizabeth confesses that she was aware of his kindness and generosity during her family's crisis. He admits that he was only thinking of her (swoon!) while he was doing this noble thing. Elizabeth is too embarrassed to speak, and so Darcy implores her to accept his proposal of marriage. She informs him that her feelings have greatly changed since she had last spoken to him. They both give an account of their own prideful and poor behavior, and it is one of the sweetest moments in all of the literature that I have read. Chapter 58, read it, and be delighted.

The next day, Darcy and Bingley are once again calling upon their lovely ladies, and after dinner, Mr. Darcy follows Mr. Bennett into his study to ask for Elizabeth's hand in marriage. He is astonished and asks Elizabeth how could this be. She explains her feelings for Mr. Darcy, and he is satisfied. She is so loved by her father, and this is such a beautiful exchange; it makes me miss my daddy all the more.

Jane and Elizabeth both marry EXCEEDINGLY well and live happily ever after.

BUT WOULD THEY?? I believe that Jane and Bingley would probably never fight, nor would they have trouble with proper marital roles. Jane would be pleasant and submissive, not needing the company of her parents or wanting to live extravagantly.

Both Elizabeth and Darcy have been greatly humbled throughout their short relationship, and one would hope that it would have a lasting effect on them; however, Elizabeth would probably question her husband's decisions and call him out any and every time that he acted in a prideful manner. We can all learn to be respectful of our husbands but still retain our fiery spirits. It would take time for Elizabeth to learn to tame her tongue and allow her husband to make an occasional mistake without feeling the need to correct him or give her advice when it hasn't been asked for. It would also be difficult to live in such a traditional home without wanting to make changes, to make it more reflective of her own tastes. She would also be living with a sister-in-law who is a teenager. This is not an easy thing, regardless of how wonderful said teenager is. Still, if I were her friend, I would tell her that it is a great thing to learn how to be a really good wife to an amazing man and that it takes patience, grace, and lots of dying to self in order to have a "perfect" blissful marriage. I DO know what I am talking about as I have lived it.

Couple Number Three: Anne Elliot and Captain Frederick Wentworth (Persuasion by Jane Austen, 1815. Best Film Version, 1995 Sony Pictures Classic)

When we first meet Anne Elliot, she is 27 years old, at the bottom of her family's pecking order, and has no one who cares for her except for her neighbor, Lady Russell, who at one time advised Anne on the matter of a proposal of marriage by Frederick Wentworth, a poor naval officer. Anne refuses the proposal but regrets the decision even so many years later. Her father and older sister are both arrogant and self-important. Her younger sister is a hypochondriac and married to another man whose proposal of marriage was refused by Anne, a Mr. Musgrove.

When the Elliot family runs out of money, they are forced from their estate in order to rent it for income. Admiral Croft and his wife, Sophia, move in, and soon enough, Sophia's brother, now a wealthy Captain Frederick Wentworth, will arrive for a visit.

In the meantime, Anne is staying with her sister, Mary, and her husband, Charles Musgrove, because Mary is feeling ill, as per usual, and always calls upon her older sister to take care of her, entertain her children, and act as a glorified mediator between Mary and her husband. They frequently visit the Main House where Charles' parents and sisters live. Soon, one of the sisters would play an important role in Anne's situation with Captain Wentworth.

Anne is informed that Captain Wentworth will soon be in the area, and on the day of his arrival at Uppercross, the Main House, Anne stays behind to care for one of Mary's injured children. She finds out that Frederick did inquire about her but as that of a slight former acquaintance, not a former love interest. Sigh!

The next morning, they see each other for the first time in over eight years!

He doesn't speak to her; he only bows, and she acknowledges him. That is it, and Anne is relieved that the worst part is over. Later, she is informed that Frederick found her to be so altered that he would not have known her. She fully realizes that her youthful beauty is gone, and she seems to be rather plain to anyone with an opinion. In her eyes, Frederick has only changed to become more glowing and manly.

Frederick has not forgiven Anne for showing what he believed was a "feebleness of character" in refusing him, an effect of over-persuasion by others. He is now rich and turned to shore from the Navy and is intent on settling down as soon as possible. He is ready to fall in love, although he has never found anyone who is Anne's equal. He desires a woman with a strong mind and with sweetness of manner. He and Anne will be thrown together quite often as Frederick becomes interested in Louisa, one of the sisters of Charles. When they meet, they barely speak, and a "perpetual estrangement" is felt by both of them. (I just love the language that Ms. Austen used! I also love the insight into Anne's thoughts whilst Frederick is speaking about his naval accomplishments as well as his acquaintance with the deceased brother of Charles Musgrove) Anne feels his "cold politeness and ceremonial grace" and is glad when he is not present. Sigh!

A few instances occur where Frederick "comes to the rescue" of Anne, but she feels that it is out of duty and gentlemanly kindness rather than out of the feeling of love or even being forgiven. She is filled with such compounding emotions that she knows not how she really feels. Frederick is becoming closer to Louisa, and she is returning his attention, so an understanding between them seems inevitable.

A trip to the sea is suggested by Frederick, and so the party arrives in Lyme, and everybody has a good time. Anne begins a friendship with another Naval Captain, a trauma-stricken man named Benwick. Their exchanges, as well as the admiring look of another gentleman, Mr. Elliot, cousin to Anne, rouse a bit of jealousy in Frederick, and one can sense a changing of the guard, so to speak. Tragedy strikes, however, as Louisa takes a life-threatening fall due to her own youthful carelessness, and Anne is the only one keeping her head about Louisa and instructing the others as to what to do to try to save her.

Anne enjoys another exchange with Captain Benwick as he accompanies her to the carriage and finds herself becoming fond of him, wondering if their acquaintance might continue. Now Anne and Frederick accompany Louisa's sister to Uppercross to summon Louisa's parents. There is a positive exchange between them as they arrive at Uppercross, with Frederick breaking the news to the parents and then returning quickly back to Lyme to check on Louisa.

Anne is now back in the company of Lady Russell, being careful not to breach the subject of Frederick Wentworth and feeling a bit awkward with nothing to do and no problems to solve. She visits the Crofts and finds that Frederick had inquired about her, making her feel very fine, indeed!

Charles and Mary return to Uppercross and, while visiting with Anne, confess that a certain Captain, Benwick to be exact, has been inquiring about her frequently, even sharing that he is reading the books that she has recommended.

Anne is reunited with her father and older sister in Bath, where they have taken up residence. Here, she finally meets her cousin, Mr. Elliot, who is supposedly in love with Anne's sister, Elizabeth. We don't believe it for a second because he is obviously attracted to Anne. In all of their meetings, they get on with each other so well that one begins to forget about Captain, whatever his name was, and put hope into this new blooming friendship.

Anne looks up her former mentor, Mrs. Smith, and learns of her tragic present life and meets the woman who nursed her back from terrible health, Nurse Rooke, whose kindness seems to have no end. (While I recall this section of the book, I imagine Anne being quite keen on becoming a nurse and friend such as Nurse Rooke.) Of course, her family scorns the friendship, except for her cousin, Mr. Elliot, who is delighted by her heartfelt kindness. He thinks of her as "a most extraordinary young woman, in her temper, manners, mind, a model of female excellence." High praise, indeed! Anne is not moved, however, by his attentions as she is unsure of his true character, former practices, and associations, giving her reasons to doubt his sincerity or ability to become head of their family one day.

Anne receives a letter from her sister, Mary, informing her that Captain Benwick and Louisa are now betrothed. Louisa has recovered and is back at Uppercross, where her fiancé will visit the next day. Anne finds this news "too wonderful for belief," and she has to remain calm so as not to incite curiosity from her father and older sister.

Anne is informed that Frederick will be in Bath shortly, and, of course, they run into each other the next day. He is more struck and confused by the sight of her than she has ever observed before. He looks quite red, while Anne feels "agitation, pain, pleasure, and something between delight and misery."

He speaks to her and turns away as if embarrassed. He comes towards her again, and this time they speak to each other. Then, seeing that sister Elizabeth has recognized him and turned away coldly, things become uncomfortable again. Still, Frederick is a gentleman and offers her anything that she might need in order to be comfortable. Then, in walks her cousin, Mr. Elliot, who whisks her away, and Anne only has time to say, "Good morning to you!" as she passes by.

Our lovers meet again at a benefit concert, where they converse for quite some time. Anne's mood is decidedly superior to all of the other people in her party, and she knows that he will find her again, yes, even look for her, before the evening is over. Anne is seated next to her cousin, Mr. Elliot, for the first act of the concert. He fills the time between movements with a lot of flattery on Anne's part, so much so that she wishes to not be near him any longer. During intermission, she is unable to rouse Frederick's attention and, after taking her seat again, is pleased to have lost the attention of Mr. Elliot. Finally, a glance from Frederick and a new conversation begins. His countenance has changed considerably, and Anne begins encouraging him until it improves; however, they are interrupted by Mr. Elliot's calling Anne to interpret some Italian song for them, and Frederick excuses himself and goes home, saying that "there is nothing worth staying here for." Anne takes this action to be jealously on Frederick's part, and her "gratification was exquisite."

The next day, Anne visits her invalid friend, Mrs. Smith, who eventually conveys to her all of the evils of her cousin, Mr. Elliot, but only after Anne repeatedly insists that she would not marry Mr. Elliot under any circumstances. Seems that Mrs. Smith is very acquainted with Mr. Elliot, and he is a wretched man without compassion, feeling, or scruples and only interested in wealth. With her suspicions confirmed, Anne returns home to think over what she has been told.

As usual, Anne is thinking of the feelings and ramifications of others involved. She does see Mr. Elliot that evening, and it is quite painful to have to speak to him, knowing what she did. Now, this particular "chapter" can be closed, and knowing that Captain Wentworth no longer has any inclinations toward Louisa, she is once again free to hope for reconciliation.

The next morning, a great surprise, sister Mary, husband Charles, Mrs. Musgrove, Henrietta, and Captain Harville (a very dear friend of Captain Wentworth's) are all in Bath for a few days, and Anne is delighted to see them. Sister Elizabeth extends an invitation for the party to spend the evening with her and her father, and all is well. Anne leaves with Mary and Charles to visit with others in the traveling party.

Anne is so kindly welcomed by everyone who knows her, except for her own father and older sister, so it is no wonder that she is drawn to this family of friends.

While Anne is visiting with Mrs. Musgrove and Henrietta, who would walk in but our dashing Captain Wentworth! Oh, but Mary, looking out the window, exclaims that she sees their cousin, Mr. Elliot, on the street. Mr. Elliot was supposed to be out of town beginning early in the morning, so when Anne corrects her sister about this, Mary becomes defensive and insists that it is indeed their cousin. Anne moves to the window and is proven to be in the wrong. Captain Wentworth looks over to Anne, and she is embarrassed, to say the least, but they have a pleasant little conversation before Anne's father and older sister appear at the inn. Anne feels an instant oppression and looks around to see that everyone else seems to feel it as well. Elizabeth acknowledges Captain Wentworth more than once and arrogantly invites everyone to "meet a few friends," instead of having a formal party at their home. Hmm. Anne promises to see everyone the next morning, and she returns home to offer assistance for the next evening's festivities.

Anne keeps her promise to spend the day with the Musgrove party, but she arrives late due to rain (I must point out that Anne would never be late for an appointment except for things beyond her control), and everyone has commenced to be present, including Captain Wentworth. Frederick had agreed to write a letter of introduction for Captain Harville, so while he was busy doing so, Captain Harville signals to Anne to join him at the window. They have a conversation about how the different sexes deal with love, unrequited or the longevity thereof, with their conversation being heard by Frederick, who is now hurriedly writing.

They leave, but Frederick returns for his gloves and draws out a letter from under the scattered paper, placing it before Anne with "eyes of glowing entreaty fixed on her for a time" and quickly leaves the room. "On the contents of that letter depended all which this world could do for her." She devoured the following words:

"I can listen no longer in silence. I must speak to you by such means as are within my reach. You pierce my soul. I am half agony, half hope. Tell me not that I am too late, that such precious feelings are gone forever. I offer myself to you again with a heart, even more your own than when you almost broke it eight years and a half ago. Dare not say that man forgets sooner than woman, that his love has an earlier death. I have loved none but you. Unjust I may have been, weak and resentful I have been, but never inconstant. You alone have brought me to Bath.

"For you alone, I think and plan. Have you not seen this? Can you fail to have understood my wishes? I had not waited even these ten days; could I have read your feelings, as I think you must have penetrated mine. I can hardly write. I am every instant hearing something which overpowers me. You sink your voice, but I can distinguish the tones of that voice when they would be lost on others. Too good, too excellent creature! You do us justice, indeed. You do not believe that there is true attachment and constancy among men. Believe it to be most fervent, most undeviating, in F.W. I must go, uncertain of my fate, but I shall return hither, or follow your party, as soon as possible. A word, a look, will be enough to decide whether I enter your father's house this evening or never." And then Jane writes, "Such a letter was not to be soon recovered from."

Swoon!

Have you ever received such a letter? I have, and she is quite correct in her statement. Anne is perceived not to be feeling well, and she is encouraged to go home. They want to call a carriage, but she will have none of it, for there is a chance of her seeing Captain Wentworth on her way home. No, the carriage is "earnestly protested against," and rightly so because as she is walking with her brother-in-law, Captain Wentworth appears. He walks silently by her side until Charles begs himself to leave for an appointment, and FINALLY, they are alone and can once again exchange those feelings and promises of their previous time, eight years prior. This time, the feelings were "happier, more tender, more tried, more fixed in a knowledge of the other's character, truth, and attachment."

She is not mistaken. Jealousy of Mr. Elliot has been the catalyst that forces Frederick to act. "Her character is now fixed on his mind as perfection itself, maintaining the loveliest medium of fortitude and gentleness." Aww, love is so wonderful, isn't it? So, they now, finally, understand each other and are betrothed. Oh, but whatever will sister Elizabeth have to say about it?

There is a very long scene in the book where Anne and Frederick talk about the past misunderstandings and reasons why things turned out as they had, but this synopsis is very long already, and the ending is the BEST!

The evening arrives with a full guest list gracing the home of Anne's father and sister, Elizabeth. Anne avoids Mr. Elliot as best she can, basking in the glow of being truly loved by all, save her father and Elizabeth, and she "has cheerful or forbearing feelings for every creature around her" and has short conversations with Captain Wentworth, one of which is wonderful, where he asks her that if he had not cut off all communication with her, would she have been open to them writing each other and keeping options open. "Would I!" is her answer, and he replies, "Good God! You would!" and he then admits that he had been too proud and hurt to ask again. Years of separation and suffering could have been spared. Oh, but would they be in this blissful state that they found themselves in had they not experienced all that life had brought before them? I think not.

The book ends by wrapping up the smaller stories by way of help given by the newly married couple, and Mr. Elliot, having now no means by which to acquire the Elliot property, leaves Bath for good.

The movie, which I love, ends quite differently with Napoleon escaping from the island of Elba and the Naval Officers being called back to sea for more war faring. Captain Wentworth's "Laconia" will make the charge with her trusty crew and a certain lady aboard. And they live happily ever after. Or will they?

One of the things that I love about Persuasion is that the difference in social status is actually favoring the female character instead of the male. It leads to less desperation on the woman's part – she can remain unmarried and still lead a well-to-do life. Anne Elliot is a very well-balanced woman, not giving heated speeches and just not talking too much. Elizabeth Bennett and Emma Woodhouse get themselves into trouble with their loquaciousness. Anne is all manners and a great listener, forgiving and compassionate, and she doesn't complain about anything. I would like to be more like her. Would she make a good wife to a prideful man who is in charge of many? Would they have well-behaved children and a home to be proud of? Would they continue their philanthropic endeavors, making the world a better place? Yes, to all of these, I say YES! What a couple for the ages! Apart from it taking almost the entire novel, as with most of Ms. Austen's, for the lovers to have a resolution, it is certainly worth the wait. Read it. Become like Anne. You won't be sorry about doing either.

Couple Number Four: Andie and Blaine (Pretty in Pink, 1986 Movie)

Andie is an adorable person who lives in the bad part of town with her mostly unemployed father. His wife, her mom, left when Andie was younger, and she is now a high school senior. She makes her own clothes and drives a beat-up pink Karmann Ghia to school. She has a best friend named Duckie, and from the looks of him, she probably made his clothes as well.

Andie attracts the attention of a rich guy named Steph, a highly arrogant, pretentious jerk who holds court with a group of his friends, one of whom is the adorable and highly sensitive Blaine, who can hardly tie his own shoes without an ok from Steph. Blaine also has a crush on Andie but keeps it a secret until one afternoon, in the computer lab, he sends Andie a cryptic message and then uses a computer trick to reveal his identity.

Andie works in a record store owned by a very eccentric woman named Iona. Blaine comes into the shop one afternoon and looks around for a bit, but really, he is there to check out Andie. He brings an album to the counter (a Steve Lawrence album), asking for her opinion on it. "It's hot, white hot!" and he says, "I'll take it." That smile and bashfulness get me every time.

Blaine returns to the store a few days later to inform Andie that he doesn't like the album he bought and then asks her to go out on a date. One of the things that I like about Andie is that she would never become something that she wasn't in order to please someone else.

On the evening of their date, Blaine is instructed to pick Andie up at the record store, and while she is waiting for him to show up, Duckie comes waltzing in to try to entice Andie to fall in love with him instead of Blaine. He lip-syncs and dances to Otis Redding's "Try a Little Tenderness," and even though he is adorable, his antics would get old pretty quickly. Andie is unmoved as well as unnerved due to Blaine's tardiness. An uncomfortable exchange with Duckie, who is hurt that she is dating someone other than him, and the actual date starts off badly when Blaine asks Andie if she wants to go home and change. "I already did," is her reply, and there is something to be said about her dress for the evening, a bit too grown up and formal. One of her cute outfits from school would have been much more appropriate for her, but she tried to dress up a little.

The first thing they do is go to a party at Steph's house. As they enter, Steph and his girlfriend Benny are dancing in their underwear, a good hint to Blaine that this is not a good idea, yet he continues to pursue this station, so he finds beer and snacks and heads upstairs to find a room. Andie protests, but Blaine sets her mind at ease, and they enter what is thought to be an empty room, but it is actually occupied by Steph and Benny (Don't ask me how they got there from downstairs so quickly), and they are invited to sit down. Benny starts putting Andie down and questioning Blaine for bringing trash to the party, so they leave.

Now you would think that two fairly intelligent people will know better, but they decide after this disaster to go to one of Andie's places, where all of her peeps like to hang out. There is a cute side story about Duckie always trying to get into the club, but the bouncer won't admit him (why Andie is allowed in and not Duckie is unclear), but this one time, Duckie is actually inside with Iona, who brought him there to try to cheer him up, telling the bouncer that Duckie was her kid. Blaine orders them a drink, and Andie joins Iona and Duckie (again, where are the brains?). On Blaine's return, Duckie gets rude and refuses to shake hands with Blaine. Duckie is hurt and jealous, so why would Andie sit with them? (Hmm, as I'm writing this, I decide that not one person in this movie is very intelligent, so why do I like it so much?) Andie and Blaine leave the club, and now Blaine says that he will take Andie home. She says no and that he can drop her off at the record store, not wanting him to know where she lives. He is confounded by this and takes her home. Out of the car, she says that maybe they shouldn't go out together; they just have too many differences. He asks her to the prom, and all is forgotten as she kisses him. (Yeah, you go, Andie! I know, I'm a fifty-eight-year-old woman writing this.)

Blaine is soon pressured by Steph to break it off with Andie.

He starts to ignore and avoid her, and she confronts him. "What about prom, Blaine?" he replies, "I asked someone before, and I forgot." (Oh, John Hughes, could you not come up with a better excuse for Blaine?) She calls him a liar, and he indeed is. There are few things worse than a person who is so afraid of what others think that they can't actually think for themselves. Andie is distraught and asks Iona to have her prom dress from her high school days. She takes it with another horrible thing that her dad picked up secondhand, and she makes herself a prom dress. She's going to walk in and walk out, not allowing them to beat her. It's a terrible dress, but Molly Ringwald looks absolutely gorgeous in it. She shows up and sees her friend Duckie dressed in his finest, and they decide to go in together. At this point, the movie could have ended as originally written, and I would have been heartbroken and completely unsatisfied that Blaine got left out in the cold. Test audiences agreed, and the cast was summoned months later to re-shoot the closing scene. Andrew McCarthy was staring on Broadway and had shaved his head for the part. They found him a terrible wig (watch the ending; you can totally tell!), and the ending was re-shot with Duckie telling Andie that Blaine had arrived and sat alone.

Blaine sees them and gets up to go to her, but Steph stops him to put that pressure on, but Blaine tells him that Andie knows that he is crap (different word used) and that deep inside, he knows she's right. (YAY, let's all clap for him!) Now that Blaine has stood his ground, he is now free to make amends at least. He says hi, and she says hi. He holds out his hand for Duckie, who hesitates but finally shakes his hand. Blaine says, "You don't need me to say I'm sorry." she says," It's done, it's over with, I'm fine." Blaine answers, "Well, if that is true, then I'm glad." Andie says, "It's not true, but it doesn't matter, does it?" And now the BEST line in the movie comes from Blaine, "You told me that you couldn't believe in someone who didn't believe in you. I believed in you, I always believed in you, I just didn't believe in me. I love you, always". (Oh, be still my heart, I love Andrew McCarthy.) Blaine walks away, and Andie is left again with Duckie, who tells her, "Andie, he came here alone, and you're right, he's not like the others" and "If you don't go to him now, I'm not going to take you to another prom again. This is an incredibly romantic moment, and you're ruining it for me, now go". Andie gives him a hug and says, "Thanks, Duckie," hurrying to the parking lot to catch Blaine. However, before that happens, we see a very cute hot chick giving Duckie the eye, and now we don't have to feel sorry for him. Andie and Blaine are reunited, they kiss, and now they live happily ever after. But wait, will these two really be able to make it as a real-life couple?

To be sure, they love each other, they're both smart and will go on to college. They have already surpassed a major hurdle in getting over peer pressure, and they are a very attractive couple. I believe, though, that they would not have a long-lasting relationship. Blaine comes from a wealthy and traditional family who will never welcome Andie into their fold. She will always be an outsider, and then there is the problem of her father, who can't hold a job and drinks too much. What would their holidays look like? Their children wouldn't be fully loved or accepted by Blaine's family, so really, the only way to reconcile all of this would be for them to both go to college, get careers of their own, and then come together not needing money from Blaine's family at all. Moving to a different state and rarely, if ever, visiting his family would help but it would always be awkward and something between them. Those of us who are dearly loved by their in-laws are truly blessed, indeed.

Couple Number Five: Birdie Pruitt and Justin Matisse (Hope Floats, 1998 Movie)

Birdie Pruitt is a sad little character who has lost her glow. Her high school heartthrob husband is having an affair with her best friend (she finds out on a talk show, which I always thought was hilarious) and decides to leave him and Chicago, takes their daughter Bernice (and I thought Adda was terrible!) and travels back to her home town in Texas to move in with her eccentric taxidermy loving mother, Ramona.

Soon enough, Ramona begins to play matchmaker with Birdie and the town's carpenter, Justin Matisse, who tried to make it in the big leagues of home building but was just too meticulous about his work, so he ended up moving back to Texas to build his own dream home. (The reason that I like Justin would be obvious to anyone who really knows me since Evan is an amazing and meticulous carpenter himself. Of course, this movie came out long before I met Evan, so what really attracts me is that he is a nice person, kind, considerate, as well as talented.)

Birdie starts to act out a little, and in my favorite scene, Justin is at the house, working, and he tells Birdie that she looks terrible and asks if she's been drinking. She comes back with, "Why do people keep asking me that? Do I have a coaster stuck to my butt or something?" She decides that she needs to get a job, so she goes to the local employment agency, run by a woman, Dot, whom Birdie never gave the time of day while in High School and who still holds a grudge. (Do people really do that? Yeah, they probably do.) So Dot sets her up with a job at a one-hour photo shop where Birdie messes up the processing machine on just about every roll of film, but she's still held on a pedestal by most people in town, so she keeps her job, all the while Justin is doing everything that he can possibly do to attract Birdie's attention and win her for himself. She needs time, and Justin has all the time in the world, so they flirt from time to time, and daughter Bernice does everything that she can to get rid of Justin because she wants her parents to reconcile. (As most children of failed marriages probably do) Bernice is funny and tragic at the same time and lends to the only other storyline that is pursued throughout.

Birdie sleeps with Justin and is regretful about it. (I was regretful about it because it doesn't need to be there and makes what could have been a perfect movie into just your normal movie without morals. Another example for me is the movie "How to Lose a Guy in 10 Days." I'll never forget going to see the movie with my youth group girls (it was rated PG), and we all walked out of the movie saying that it would have been perfect had the main characters not had sex. That was a proud Mama Adda moment. Back to Birdie and Justin, she tells him that she's not ready, but he is there for her when her mother passes away and is also a great friend to Birdie's little nephew, who has been abandoned by Birdie's sister. It is all very promising.

The movie ends with the new little family unit walking together at a carnival. Bernice asks Birdie if she is going to marry Justin. Birdie says, "Oh honey, I don't think I'll get married for quite some time. Why you don't like Justin?" Bernice replies, "It's not that. I just don't want to be known as Bernice Matisse!"

As they walk toward home, with the Bryan Adams song, "When You Love Someone," in the background, Birdie takes Justin's hand, and they live happily ever after. Or would they? Why yes, I think they would!

Some may consider this movie to be a bit boring and contrived, but I think that the characters are well-written, and the story is believable. Birdie was the most popular person in town as a high schooler, and she marries the Football Hero Quarterback, who isn't really a nice, caring person. Birdie is completely humiliated on national television and needs to be loved and cared for by someone who is nice and caring. Justin is those things and more. He is talented, responsible, a good father figure, and willing to be patient while the girls are healing. He will be an asset instead of a hindrance.

If you are married to a nice guy, be nice back and be careful not to fall into the trap of being disrespectful to him, or any type of husband for that matter. Respect and appreciation are paramount to a man's emotional well-being in the marriage and will certainly fill him with much love for his wife. Don't agree? Read the excellent book, "Love and Respect" by Emerson Eggerichs, and what I am saying will make total sense. I have seen many marriages healed and restored just by making a few simple changes in behavior and belief outlined in this book.

Happy Reading.

Couple Number Six: Baby Houseman and Johnny Castle (Dirty Dancing, 1987 Movie)

When Dirty Dancing premiered in 1987, I was 23 years old, single, living with my mom and little sister in a trailer park (echoes of childhood), and working in a video store. I had only dated a few guys since moving to Southern California from Fort Morgan, Colorado, and not one of them was a good fit. In fact, I was beginning to believe that I couldn't fit with anyone on the planet, so I loved movies, especially the ones about misfits trying to find love. Romancing the Stone was a favorite because the woman was a writer and didn't know much about the world around her. I had always wanted to be a writer, and when I arrived in California, I was as naive as they come. Funny story: my first real job after moving to So. Cal was in a video store (not the one that I would work at for 17 years of my life), and the owner was this off the wall guy named Charlie. If he saw you and didn't insult you, it meant that he didn't like you and didn't want to waste time speaking to you. If he did insult you, you knew that you had made a friend. Well, on my first day, Charlie was showing me what my job would be, and he pointed at some video covers and said that these ones go in this special room over here. I asked why, and he said that they are movies of an "adult nature." I looked at one of the boxes, and it was a pornographic movie!! I turned fifty shades of red and didn't even want to touch the boxes, let alone go into a room full of them. Talk about sheltered upbringing; I knew that there were magazines of this nature, but movies?

Back to Dirty Dancing. I am a realist by nature, so some stories are just too out there to be believable, and this movie, though I enjoy it, is one of those pretty unbelievable romances. Before you try to talk me into believing it, let me tell you why this is a very unlikely coupling as far as making it to living happily ever after.

Baby Houseman is seventeen years old and will most certainly go to college, just like her idolized Daddy did. She wants to join the Peace Corps and make a difference in the world. She will have the ability to have everything that she dreams of because her family is wealthy. She is vacationing with her family at an upscale resort for the summer.

In contrast, Johnny Castle (hilarious name) is the resort's dance instructor who looks over thirty, but I believe in the story, he is supposed to be about twenty-five. He has been around this scene for quite some time and is very rough around the edges. The chip on his shoulder weighs a ton, and he never really knows where his next job will come from. We learn very little about his history or where that chip came from. Baby and Johnny meet when Baby is enlisted by another resort employee to help carry refreshments to a secret hideout where other employees go to engage in their "dirty dancing." Baby's first reaction to her surroundings is shock, then curiosity, and ends with being awestruck by the last couple to enter the room, Johnny and Penny. Johnny sees Baby and asks his cousin, "What's she doing here?" Baby's first words to Johnny? "I carried a watermelon." I know, I didn't write it.

Johnny and Penny are required, for reasons stated but unclear, to dance at an exhibition at a nearby hotel, but Penny is unable to perform (I won't go into why), so Baby is once again enlisted to help. The dance teaching sequences between Johnny and Baby are sweet and funny. Their performance goes off with a few hitches but is good enough.

Baby and Johnny continue to meet in secret for most of the remaining story because they are in love. Why in secret, you ask? Because if Dr. Houseman knew what his favorite girl was up to, she would no longer occupy the pedestal that he had placed her on. Ideals and morality were different back in the early sixties, and an unmarried teenager being sexually active was not something to brag about, not to mention that the age difference between the characters is pretty substantial.

The movie ends with the famous line from Johnny to Dr. Houseman, "Nobody puts Baby in a corner," and the last dance of the summer with Baby finally dancing to perfection to the song, (I've Had) "The Time of My Life," and they lived happily ever after. Hmm, could they?

Not a chance; even the song points to a goodbye for our lovers. Baby will go to college, and Johnny will move on to the next gig. As a couple who probably shouldn't have coupled in the first place, it made for a nice movie, but not at all believable.

Couple Number Seven: Kathleen Kelly and Joe Fox (You've Got Mail, 1998 Movie)

This story is a classic, and I mean LITERALLY a classic. The play, Parfumerie, was written in 1937 and made into a movie, "The

Shop Around the Corner," with one of my favorites, Jimmy Stewart, and Margaret Sullivan, who is NOT a favorite. I always thought that they would never make it as a couple because she was just too toxic a personality, especially for Jimmy Stewart, who can do no wrong in my mind. Next, it was made into a musical with Judy Garland, which doesn't interest me at all, and finally, it was made into one of the best romantic comedies EVER, "You've Got Mail."

This version has a different twist in that instead of the couple working in the same place and hating each other, they are both in the book business. Joe Fox would inherit a very large fortune and book conglomerate, simply called 'Fox Books," with stores on every corner. Kathleen continues to run a business called "The Shop Around the Corner," created by her amazing Mother, who has passed away. Kathleen's shop is intimate, sophisticated, and family-oriented. Fox Books resembles the large chain book stores, like Barnes and Noble, perceived by Kathleen and her staff as being impersonal and maybe even a little evil as they are systematically putting other bookstores out of business.

They first "meet" in a chat room online. When this movie was released in 1998, not every home in America had a personal computer. I didn't even own a computer until I got married in 2004, so the thought of having cyber mail was still a relatively new thing. If you had AOL as your internet provider, whenever you had an e-mail, you would hear the slogan "You've Got Mail" and be excited to read your messages. If you didn't hear it, you would probably be a little sad that you had received no messages. This is, of course, long before junk mail became prevalent.

Kathleen and Joe are both in unsatisfying relationships with narcissists, so their joining chatrooms online isn't surprising; however, they keep their newfound correspondence secret. Her screen name is "Shop Girl," and he is "NY152".

They refuse to give personal information, such as real names, where they live, work, etc. Each is enjoying just having someone to talk to about how their day is going and how they feel about the world around them. When they try to talk to their live-in partners, they are shut down because what that person has to say is always more important.

Fox Books acquires a property just down the street from Kathleen's shop and announces the opening of their new store. Kathleen tries to remain positive, but deep down, she worries about losing her mother's legacy. It's hard to imagine, from a realistic point of view, how Kathleen could survive, living in the Upper West Side of Manhattan with only a small book business for income. (It doesn't matter, Adda, it's a movie!)

Their first face-to-face meeting occurs at "The Shop Around the Corner," where Joe has brought his much younger Aunt and brother for a story hour. Knowing that his family will put her out of business soon, Joe will only reveal his first name to Kathleen while his young brother spells out FOX when Kathleen asks him to spell "cat." Kathleen fails to put the two together, so when they meet again at a party, Kathleen finds out that he is, in fact, Joe Fox, the man who is about to make her life miserable. They have a spat about several different matters, such as caviar being a garnish and having been properly introduced, can now put a face to their respective antagonists.

They continue to see each other in various places in their neighborhood, and in one instance, Joe comes to her rescue when she gets into the wrong line at the grocery store. Zip Zip. The other times, they try to hide so as not to be seen by the other. The Christmas sequence is especially sad. Kathleen is missing her mother and worrying about losing her business, so she reaches out to her screen beau, NY152, for business advice.

He tells her that she needs to "go to the mattresses," a wonderful reference to "The Godfather," my absolute favorite movie, meaning to go to war. He also quotes some other parts of the movie because "you can find the answer to any question in The Godfather." What should I pack for my Summer vacation? "Leave the gun, take the cannoli." What day of the week is it? "Monday, Tuesday, Thursday, Wednesday".

So, Kathleen enlists the help of her boyfriend and a well-known children's author for a smear campaign in the press against big business, especially that of the Fox Family. They call each other some names and remain in a tug-of-war match, which we all know will end in defeat for Kathleen.

NY152 declares to Shop Girl that they should "meet" in person, but this goes nowhere until Kathleen is desperate. She asks if he still wants to meet her. They agree to meet at a cafe where she will be holding a copy of Pride and Prejudice and a single rose. The Jane Austen book comes up several times during the movie, which I love, of course. Joe arrives at the cafe with his friend and asks the friend to see if she is there and if she's pretty. He says that she is and that she looks a lot like Kathleen Kelly. Joe sees Kathleen and is disappointed and still a little bitter about the bad press that he received, so he goes into the cafe, but not as NY152, but as himself. He ends up sitting behind her, antagonizing her, and she following up with insults toward him.

Broken-hearted, Kathleen messages NY152, insisting that he must have had a good reason not to be there. Joe contemplates whether to respond. He comes up with some lies but keeps erasing them, eventually sending her a heartfelt apology, which reopens the line of communication between them. This is a turning point for Joe as he is now feeling compassion for Kathleen and wants her to know him as himself and fall in love with him.

Both Kathleen and Joe break up with their respective partners, leaving an opening for someone new. Now, we get to witness a perfect little setup for romance as the two become friends; however, Kathleen is still pining for NY152. She messages him that they should meet, and he tells her that he wants to meet but is in the middle of a project that needs "tweaking." He plays a game, writing to her in the evening while during the day trying to steer her away from the make-believe person and into the real one. Their banter is wonderful and makes me smile every time I see the movie. I never get tired of it.

NY152 writes to Shop Girl that it is time to meet in a beautiful garden spot and that he will bring Brinkley, his wonderful Golden Retriever. As Joe and Kathleen meet for lunch, she informs him that she is finally meeting NY152, and on their way back to her place, they talk about what could have happened had their circumstances been different. You want them to kiss right then and forget about the meeting in the park, but that would take away one of the best movie endings EVER.

Kathleen arrives early, and NY152 doesn't seem to be there. She is worried that she will be stood up again when suddenly she hears a man calling out, "Brinkley!" and she sees him walking toward her. Many emotions appear on her face: joy, disbelief, hurt, and as she cries, he wipes her tears and says, "Don't cry, Shop Girl, don't cry." Then she declares that she wanted it to be him so badly. Then they kiss, pet the dog, and live happily ever after! Or could they possibly? Of COURSE!

The hard part is already over. They know the worst and best things about each other. She will be able to start a new career or maybe have children and spend her life being a mom and homemaker. If they fought, they would forgive and make up quickly. She might get a bit tired of his antics, but I am married to a funny guy, and I don't get tired of him. (Sometimes his humor is just timed badly, but it is never meant to hurt or frustrate me.) They would never want for anything, being rich and in perfect love, and I believe that they really would live happily ever after.

Honorable Mention

Other Couples Who Really Could Live Happily Ever After

*Bob and Grace (Return to Me, 2000 Movie)

*Mr. Knightly and Emma (Emma, 1815 Novel. Best Movie Version 1996)

*Harry and Sally (When Harry Met Sally, 1989 Movie) or literally ANY romantic comedy coupling that includes Meg Ryan (i.e., Sleepless in Seattle, IQ, Addicted to Love, French Kiss, Kate and Leopold, etc)

*Ronny and Loretta (Moonstruck, 1987 Movie)

*Lloyd and Diane (Say Anything, 1989 Movie)

*Benjamin and Andie (How to Lose a Guy in 10 Days, 2003 Movie)

*Jake and Samantha (Sixteen Candles, 1984 Movie)

*Jack and Lucy (While You Were Sleeping, 2007 Movie)

*Will and Skylar (Good Will Hunting, 1997 Movie)

*Alex and Isabel (Fools Rush In, 1997 Movie)

*Westley and Buttercup (The Princess Bride, 1987 Movie)

*Pat and Tiffany (Silver Linings Playbook, 2012 Movie)

Couples Who Would Never Make It

*Rhett and Scarlett (Gone With The Wind, 1936 Novel, 1939 Movie)

*Edward and Vivian (Pretty Woman, 1990, Movie) or literally ANY coupling that includes Julia Roberts (i.e. Mystic Pizza, Runaway Bride, Notting Hill, Ticket to Paradise, etc)

*Charles and Carrie (Four Weddings and a Funeral, 1994 Movie)

*George and Lucy (Two Weeks Notice, 2002 Movie)

*Ian and Toula (My Big Fat Greek Wedding, 2002 Movie)

*Steve and Mary (The Wedding Planner, 2001 Movie) or literally ANY coupling that includes Jennifer Lopez (i.e., Maid in Manhattan, Monster-in-Law, Gigli, Jersey Girl, etc)

*Walter and Hildy (His Girl Friday, 1940 Movie)

*Jake and Jane (It's Complicated, 2009 Movie)

*Danny and Sandy (Grease, 1978 Movie)

*Han and Leia (Star Wars, 1977 Movie)

*Mark and Bridget (Bridget Jones's Diary 2001 Movie)

*Allie and Noah (The Notebook, 2004 Movie)

These and other couples COULD be featured in a future publication.

Rude Awakenings

"Mrs. Joe was a very clean housekeeper, but had an exquisite art of making her cleanliness more uncomfortable and unacceptable than dirt itself." (Great Expectations, Charles Dickens 1860)

I love this quote, from one of my favorite tales, for it aptly describes my initial transition from single living to married life. In my mind, everything has a place and everything should be returned to it's said place as soon as it is no longer needed. When you live alone it is entirely possible to have one's space be organized and uncluttered but when you have housemates it is nearly impossible.

I had never had a "roommate" in all the years that I lived on my own. I had been blessed to know people who had rooms or apartments to rent at very low prices so the need was never there. I cherished having my own space and only myself to answer to.

Evan had been married before and, right out of high school, so he had never lived alone. The transitional hardships, if any, would all be on me. Even living with a teenager, no matter how wonderful, was going to be a huge change for me because I knew that I couldn't just go into the situation and try to force my will on everyone. This was an established home and any changes would have to be talked through and agreed upon before undertaking.

This all meant that I would have to change my "great expectations" into realistic ones. Since appearances didn't matter much to Evan or Ashley I realized that I was really only cleaning for myself so huffing and puffing about it all of the time would not have the desired effect that I would want it to. As a matter of fact, men don't get our hints, as a general rule (neither do teenagers, of either gender). If we want something from our men it is always best to tell them, straight out, what it is. It would take me a long time to learn this lesson.

But I DID learn this and other very helpful lessons from the many marriage books we read, and used for classes and one-to-one counseling, when we started a couples ministry at Centerpoint. Most were Christian-based but there was one, "The Seven Principles for Making Marriage Work" (Dr. John Gottman and Nan Silver, 2015), that is based on science and has an invaluable section filled with practical exercises for couples to go through together.

Other notable titles: the aforementioned "The Five Love Languages", and 'Love and Respect", "Men are Like Waffles Women are Like Spaghetti" (Bill and Pam Ferrell, 2007), "From Anger to Intimacy" (Dr. Gary Chapman and Ted Cunningham, 2009), and "The Four Seasons of Marriage" (Dr. Gary Chapman, 2012).

Everything that I learned and put into practice made my marriage experience better and I highly recommend them, even if your marriage is great, the information is enlightening and can only make your relationship stronger and more fulfilling.

There were many other transitional areas that I would have to face: My desire to "nest" and make the home reflect my own personal style would have to wait for quite a few years to come to fruition. In the meantime we decided on a style that fit both of us, mostly centered around artwork that we purchased together.

When I was single, I got paid monthly so my bills were all paid at the beginning of the month. Evan likes to pay bills on the date that they are due. I lived on a strict budget but Evan didn't believe that a self employed person could live on a budget. My bank account was closed and then we had two, one for Evan's business and a joint personal one. How much and how often I could spend had to become a joint decision. I was thirty-nine. This was hard. It would become an issue later on, because of my inability or reluctance to voice my feelings. Many years of being silent about things that bothered me cost me a great deal including developing acid reflux and muscle myalgia. Evan finally told me that he was a big boy and could handle whatever it was that was bothering me so would I please talk to him. Trust is so important, especially in marriage, and he has never reacted poorly when I have shared something and I have become better about sharing right away instead of holding all of my feelings inside and suffering in silence.

I like to sleep in and Evan is an early riser so I needed to adapt to a schedule more like his, however, I still find it difficult to go to bed before ten o'clock and Evan falls asleep on the couch as early as eight. Movie watching is rarely successful in the evening for this reason.

When we first got married I would get up earlier than usual on Saturdays so that we could watch one of my many movies that Evan had never seen, or even heard of. I loved introducing him to Jimmy Stewart, Cary Grant, Gary Cooper, Bogart, and Brando. He appreciated the wonderful storytelling of a bygone era of Hollywood along with the skills of the actors involved.

One particular Saturday morning, Evan told me that he was hungry and wanted to go to breakfast. Would I be willing to just put up my hair and get dressed quicky so that we could leave shorty? Evan loves to be spontaneous and "fly by the seat of his pants" (his term for this state of being) and I once heard about people who were spontaneous but I spurned the practice. I did relent, however, and now I am surprised at how I will go out of the house looking sometimes. All because he wanted breakfast.

My cooking skills were minimal, at first, but I had learned quite a lot from Mom while growing up so I knew what to do but hadn't had much practice putting meals together or shopping for more than just myself. As a single person I would just pick up takeout or go to dinner with friends. Now I took it upon myself to plan and implement what we would have for dinner on any given night and it was stressful because I was working until five o'clock, or later, and everyone was usually hungry when I got home. I hate waking up to messes so I made a rule that whoever cooks needs to clean up afterward. This worked well since I cooked most of the time. When Ashley cooked she did her best to clean up and even though it wasn't my kind of clean I appreciated her attempts. Dishes WOULD end up being a point of contention between us throughout the years that she lived at home with us. I'll never forget the day that she cleaned out her room, unearthing several bowels and plates containing fossilized food, and after putting them in the kitchen sink to deal with later, left to go hang out with some friends. I got home and wasn't happy about said dishes so I put them in a large bowel and put them back into her room. This one act would turn out to be the straw that broke the back of a sweet teenager, resulting in her moving out shortly after and would never live with us again. The things that you cannot take back or undo…

Pets, and my need to have them, would become a minor point of contention that has lasted through the duration of our marriage. Marrying me was a package deal, with a cat named Millie included. For all of our years together I have never lasted for more than a few months between the demise of one pet and the acquisition of another. Poo Poo Kitty had to be laid to rest about a year after we got married and so I was considering what to do about our pet vacancy very early on. Evan would be happier if we had never adopted ANY pets. He doesn't see or feel the need for them, they cramp his style and cost him money.

I don't have biological children so having a pet helps me to quiet the maternal instinct that lives inside of me. I asked Evan if he would rather I exercise these instincts with him, there by treating him like a child and his resounding answer was "no" so when I had grieved for a few months I decided that I wanted another cat and would name him Rascal. Now, I just needed to find him.

When you adopt from a rescue they usually have a lot of stipulations that you have to agree to in order to adopt. I loved going to Pet Smart because they always had cats and you could go in and play with them and hold them to see if they would be a good fit. I went in, one day, and there just happened to be a cat there named Rascal! He was really cute, and loving. I called the number to talk to the rescue place and she came down to talk to me and we were just getting ready to do the deal when I read the clause about not willingly or routinely allowing the animal to go outside. I was sad because I really wanted him but I don't like having to force a cat to remain indoors all of it's life, unless it actually CHOOSES to. I would much rather have a happy animal who has freedom over an unhappy one stuck inside. I've had to pay dearly for this in that I lost several animals to coyotes and one hit by a car. In this case, I had to move on because I wouldn't sign the agreement knowing that I would allow the animal to go outside if it wanted to. So my search continued.

Our nearby shelter didn't have any kittens so I checked another animal store in the area. Elliot's Pets it was called and when I walked in I heard the familiar sound of kittens playing and hissing and meowing. I walked up to the cage and this adorable little tabby approached me and started to purr. I opened the cage, took him out and adopted him right then. I named him Rascal, of course, and he really lived up to the name! He hardly ever calmed down, even to eat or sleep and since we were gone quite a bit Evan suggested getting him a playmate. Yes, you heard me right, EVAN suggested it! SO we went back to Elliot's and adopted a funny looking little guy that we called Charlie. Evan preferred to call him Charles because he said that he looked like a proper gentleman. Not long after we had Charlie he decided to pee on Evan while we were sleeping. Apparently, he had wanted to snuggle during the night but was rejected. "That's two!", Evan proclaimed! It wouldn't be the last.

My two boys were happy and healthy and always wanted to go outside right after breakfast (we fed them the meow mix pouches and Rascal would stick his whole face into the food and get it all over himself every time he ate. He didn't ever cover up his poo poo in the litter box and if you have ever had a kitten you know how badly their poo poo smells) so on one particular day, when they were about eighteen months old, I let them out and we never saw Charlie again. Evan went out to look for him and found his collar as well as his very distinctive looking tail, so we knew what happened to him. As much as I had hoped that they would stay close to the house he had wandered off to a dangerous place. We missed him and his great personality but Rascal was especially upset about him, constantly walking around meowing as if to call him home. We thought about getting another one but a chance to help someone that I love made it un-necessary.

My Cousin, Debbie, called begging me to take her cat, Peanut, off of her hands because she and her husband were both battling cancer and just couldn't take care of him any longer. So I talked to Evan about it and we agreed to keep him. Peanut was a man's kind of cat, loyal and affectionate but not too clingy. When we first brought him home he lived behind our washer and dryer only emerging when it was time to eat or get a drink. This lasted for about a month and he finally allowed us to pet him so we closed off the laundry room and made him a bed in the hall closet, where he lived for another month all the while getting to know us and Rascal. Soon he was in our bedroom, behind my dresser, for another month. One night he decided to get up on our bed and pee on Evan. Yes, it really did happen again! Why did they always pee on Evan and not on me? Hmm.

Never did figure out that one. Eventually Peanut became a wonderful addition to our home, a cuddle buddy to Rascal and preferring Evan's company above the rest of us he spent much of his time in whatever room Evan happened to be in.

Rascal, on the other hand, was still living up to his given name and we had a great deal of fun playing with him and scaring him so that he would jump from all fours, straight up, and land wherever his flight took him. I let him out one morning and never saw him again. We went and looked for him, I asked all of our neighbors if they had seen him. Evan checked the field behind our house, where we found Charlie, but there was no sign of him. I cried for weeks over him. Two years wasn't long enough to have him but he had been a very happy cat and my hope has always been that he just found a new home, since he was extremely friendly and beautiful too.

Now we just had Peanut who was perfectly content with being the only animal in the house but I wanted at least one more cat, now that I was so used to having two. I decided that I would adopt again and his name would be Tucker. Evan said that this was a terrible idea and wouldn't I wait for a while before making the decision? Ok, I agreed to wait for a while but I didn't change my mind, I still wanted to get a kitten and name him Tucker, I just had to bide my time.

Later, whenever I would mention adopting another pet, Evan would want me to wait a bit longer and so, as not to be a source of friction, I waited. My birthday was coming up so I was asked for suggestions on what we should do to celebrate. This kept my thoughts occupied and so on my special day I received a card from Evan that was inscribed, "and for your Birthday, go and find Tucker" and that is what I did.

My first stop was Elliot's Pets. I walked straight to the kitten cage and this little tan tabby jumped onto the side of the cage and just hung there crying, begging me to choose him. I opened the cage and brought him out. He was really small and liked to be held. I got a feather toy to play with him but he didn't respond. Disappointed, I promptly put him back into the cage and shut the door. Again he grabbed onto the side of the cage and cried loudly. Not seeing any other kittens that interested me I said, "alright, I guess YOU found me" and took him home.

Peanut didn't like him, at first, especially because the first thing that Tucker did was go to him and start "nursing" off of his neck. Poor guy, we started calling him Mommy Peanut, he would have to hide or get up really high in order to shake Tucker off.

We had only had Tucker for a few weeks when he started sneezing and wheezing. He also had something going on with his ears so we took him in and he was given drops for his ears and liquid antibiotics. He didn't get better, even after several rounds of treatment. His cough got worse and I got worried. Evan said that we got a lemon and should take him back. My friend Nancy told me to take him to her vet and so we started on a different protocol, three more times, and he was still not getting better.

On the last visit, his Dr. said that there was one other thing to try, and it would either cure him or kill him so we took a chance and he finally got better. Great, and it only cost about a thousand dollars to get him well! Poor Evan, the last thing in the world he wanted to do was to spend his hard earned cash on an animal, especially a cat. Probably due to his illness, Tucker preferred to be safe in the house and Peanut was afraid to go out as well, so no more worrying about my "children" being outdoors and in danger. This was good.

In 2009, Evan was embarking on a new venture, entering into the world of fine art, that would take him to distant places as well as needing extra time to create new pieces. He agreed to consider getting me a puppy for constant companionship. I did a lot of research and decided on getting a poodle mix since they don't shed and are hypoallergenic. With two cats already, there was plenty of hair floating around so I thought this would help to keep the cleaning of said hair to a minimum. My first choice was a cockapoo and then a golden doodle. I found out that these poodle mixes were considered "designer dogs" and could be pretty expensive so I was hesitating to bring it up. Funny thing how God can bring things up for us.

We were going to the mall to find Evan some nice shirts to wear for his upcoming gallery debut and for the Art Walk nights that he would need to attend. Whenever we would go to the mall on previous occasions, we would always park in the back of the mall, near the JC Penny's store. This particular time Evan decided to park in the parking garage. I asked him why but he offered no explanation.

We walked into the mall and immediately to my right was a store called "Bark Works" and it was FILLED with every designer dog that I had researched, and more. I saw the Golden doodle, labradoodle, aussiepoo, and a sweet cockapoo. This adorable guy started licking the glass to get my attention and he just smiled at me. I instantly fell in love and decided that I would name him Henry. However, when I asked how big he would get, it turned out that he would not be a lap sized boy so I kept looking.

In one of the cages there was a little gray girl who seemed really sad. I looked at the breed information, a Schnoodle, and realized that I hadn't heard of that one so I knew nothing about it. Evan noticed her too; she wouldn't even look at us, just laid there.

We left the store, did our shopping and on our way out, I wanted to stop back at the puppy store and get the name of that breed again as I had quickly forgotten it. We walked right up to the cage and the sweet thing still had her head buried and hadn't touched her dinner. Evan spoke first, "Do you want to see her?" I said, "Do I !" and we went into a small room and waited for the trainer to bring her in. I sat on the floor, Evan on the bench. The door opened, she let go of the leash and the puppy ran into my arms and started kissing my face. Evan didn't say a word, he just got up and paid.

I named her "Pepper" right then and we took her to her forever home. She has been a joy to me all of these 14 years and the constant companion that I had wished for.

We had other kittens, over the years. There was Jack, who I found at Pet Smart, and he was such a beautiful boy, I really wanted him. Evan said that I was out of my mind and why did I need yet another animal to take care of. I was persistent and so a few days later I picked him up and he was THE best cat I had ever had. He didn't do anything wrong and even Pepper liked him. I now had my four "children" and all was grand, until we went away for a weekend ministry trip.

We left on Friday, and everyone was well and happy. Janice housesat for us and always took great care of my babies so I had no worries at all. When we returned Sunday night, Jack didn't look well. Janice said that he had been fine all weekend but he wouldn't eat that night so I was a bit concerned. The next morning he looked worse and tried to eat but would just vomit after trying so I made an appointment for him. After an exam they took a sample of fluid from his abdomen and by the look of it, determined that he had a corona virus, probably from birth, and that there was no other way to know about it except with a blood test so it wouldn't be fair to blame the rescue for giving me a sick animal. They offered to "take care of him" meaning to put him down for me, but I took him home to be with me. They said it would take about a week so I stayed with him, giving him small amounts of water and lots of love. They were correct, it took a week and I cried like I had never cried before. Evan buried him in the back yard, wrapped in a special little blanket.

It is always so difficult to lose one of them and Jack had only been eleven months old so this was especially hard. I resigned myself to having three pets, for a time, until a young adult girls hangout one afternoon called for a trip to Pet Smart to look at the rescues there. It wasn't even initiated by me, really!

I could tell that he was a little stinker from the moment we walked in. He was doing somersaults in the cage and knocked both the food and water bowls over. Oh, I liked him. Just like the 6th and 7th grades that I loved teaching the bible to, he was obnoxious but funny. I sent his photo to Evan, and again, he tried to talk me out of it. I gave it a few days and then I went back to the store, found the adoption lady, Ruth, and told her that I wanted to adopt another kitten. When I told her which one she informed me that he and his cage mate had just been adopted that morning. I was really sad. I didn't even go and look at the others, there was just something about that one that I loved.

I am not normally sentimental or melancholy but this really broke my heart and I cried, as though grieving the loss of something important. When I told Evan that he had already been adopted there was a slight smile on his face, as though he were thinking, "thank you, Lord, for intervening" and we didn't talk about it again.

A few weeks later, I went into the same store to get food for Pepper (She is allergic to corn so we had to find her food that she could tolerate) and Ruth was there. She said hello and that she was just getting ready to call me. It seemed that the man who had adopted the two kittens was arrested and his girlfriend had the kittens scanned to see where they had originated from. The rescue picked them up, isolated them for a bit and brought them back to the store to get them re- adopted. She asked if I was still interested. Of course I was, but then she said that since they had been together for so long, they would like them to be adopted together again.

I said that I couldn't do that and expect to have a home to go back to (ha!) so I was sad again. She said to give it a few weeks and if they weren't adopted by then, she would let me have the one that I wanted. I had already decided to name him Riley and those two weeks seemed like six months but I did wait the full two weeks. I only went to the store once to see if they were still there. Really, it was only once! Finally the day arrived and I went to the store and they were still there. I called Ruth and she came down to meet me and sign the paperwork. Again, I was adopting a rescue animal, and like Jack, I planned to keep Riley in the house.

To say that I went from the best cat to the worst one is an understatement. I have never had an animal test my limits like Riley did, his first year with me. He got into EVERYTHING; slept on my dinning room table, knocked things off of my counters, ruined my expensive curtains, went poo poo in my large plants, fought with and had to dominate all of my other animals, and was not a lap cat. The things that I found adorable while he was incarcerated weren't so adorable when he was ruining things and I was catching flack from my husband. Something had to give and Evan suggested that we just let him outside or we take him back where I got him. I didn't want to do that so I reluctantly let him out.

That first day he rewarded me with a small gopher, which he kept throwing up into the air to get my attention to the back door where I would see it. He then proceeded to eat the thing, and I mean the WHOLE thing, then he wanted to come inside for a nap. One time he grabbed a gopher along with a few springs of jasmine and brought them home. So, that morning he brought me a gopher AND flowers! He slept until the next morning and after that, he never misbehaved again, unless you consider bringing live gophers into your house to play with, until dead, and then feasting on them misbehaving!

In 2017, we went on a road trip to the Pacific Northwest. The morning of our trip, I called for Riley to come in, to say goodbye but he didn't come. I never saw him again. He had sometimes stayed out the whole night so I hadn't been too concerned the night before. One has to put that heartache away somewhere so as to still have a meaningful time on vacation. Niki was sitting the house for us and she and her boyfriend looked for him while we were gone. Our friend Gary looked for him too.

I still miss that crazy cat. We started calling him "Hannibal Lector" because he always ate his kills and had an insatiable desire to kill things. We also lost Peanut, a year earlier, to kidney failure. He was a sweet boy.

One time while I was spending the day with Mom she told me that she wanted either a kitten or a baby, and since I couldn't help her with the baby thing, I said that I could help her get a kitten. Art wasn't thrilled about it but he rarely denied Mom anything, so we went to the rescue place and found a cute little orange tabby and took him to Mom and Art's.

He liked to snuggle but he was a kitten and kittens like to cause trouble. He was doing all of the bad things that kittens do and so a few weeks later I got a call from Mom asking me if I would come and get the kitten. They had named him Tiger but we decided to call him Charlie instead. He just looked like a Charlie, and he was every bit as terribly behaved as Riley was. He would wait for any opportunity to rush out the door and succeeded quite a few times. One time I got a call from my neighbor Helen, she had captured him on her porch and was holding him inside her house. I gratefully picked him up and he got out again a few weeks later.

I waited and waited for him to come home and he finally did, bringing the gift of a very small squirrel which he had killed and left at the door for me. He didn't like to eat his kills so I gave him dinner. He would escape many more times, even though we were careful not to leave the doors open for long, and one day he didn't come home. I looked for him, kept calling him but he didn't come. Evan told me to look behind the house, as he had seen him back there a few times. Well, he WAS there, and he had died, probably from a car hitting him. He had dragged himself home but couldn't get over the wall. He'd had such a short life.

I would not get another animal, at this time, because we were in the process of leaving California. Tucker was getting old and he wasn't doing all that well. He was having some of the same problems that Peanut had gone through. Just after we got me moved to Washington, his kidneys failed and I had to put him down. Evan was still in Cali so I had to grieve alone. He was my sweet cuddle buddy for over fourteen years. I still miss him.

About a month later, I told Evan that I wanted to get a kitten. I am a cat person, if you hadn't guessed and I'm not really happy unless I have at least one so I started the adoption process, as it is done in our new town. I filled out an application and kept looking at the available cats on the website.

I found the one that I wanted so I called and made an appointment to visit and meet him. I went into the place and talked with a shelter volunteer about him and as I walked over to a little bench and sat down, this tiny little guy came over to me. I picked him up and he started purring, loudly. I asked her if this was Samuel and she said that he was. I was getting ready to go to the other room when another adorable kitten walked toward me. As she was walking she kept doing this thing where she would spin her head down and around several times and then rub herself on my pant leg. I asked if they were siblings, since they were the same age, size and had similar markings. Yes, they were siblings so I decided to take them both, and right there I named them Benny and Joon.

They are perfect and even Evan has to admit that Joonie is probably the most precious thing on earth. She is fierce and likes to kill things. Benny is the love bug. He purrs as soon as I walk into a room with him and loves to sleep in my lap, although he is so big now that he hardly fits. The word "NO" means nothing to him and if I don't do whatever it is that he wants me to do he will jump onto my side table and start knocking things off. He's a brat but gets away with it. Joonie likes to sleep on Evan's lap and does her little "one two" thing with her head whenever she sees one of us approaching her. She also likes cheese, an awful lot, and jumps onto the bar or counter top to do her "one two" and kiss our faces so that we will give in and give her some shredded cheese. She will do this ten times in a day and will have success about half the time. It doesn't take much for me to give in to her and she really is a good cat, behavior wise. Certainly better than her brother. I sometimes refer to them as my hooligans and they do live up to the title.

We are now settled, in Washington, with two cats in the yard and a doodle who goes for walks around the neighborhood. Oh, and we acquired a cat named Sherbert, he came with the house. Nothing else is needed.

Part Three

Oh, The Places We've Gone

Adventures With Babysitting

Like any other pet owner, our adventures required us to find suitable help in minding the fort while we were away. For the first few years, Janice would kindly agree to stay with them, partly because this gave her a chance to have some alone time as she was a live-in nanny caring for two children and keeping an entire household in order. These were like vacations for her. After that, we had an ongoing plethora of suitable young adults who would gladly volunteer, and all that was needed was some cash and lots of junk food in the pantry. You never realize how blessed you are until you no longer have this plethora of suitable sitters. The ability to vacation worry-free should never be taken for granted.

These days, we have an RV trailer, so when we travel, we all make the trips, and it is much easier. Well, don't ask Benny and Joon if they agree because they absolutely HATE being cooped up in the RV. We have even had a few close calls with Joonie escaping and not coming back to the campsite until four in the morning, with Evan sitting outside waiting for her. Upon writing this, it has been over a year since we have been able to take out the RV. I wonder how they will respond next time since they are older and a little better behaved. We will see about that.

We have taken so many road trips, and I highly recommend all of these places if you ever have the ability to travel. Our favorite places have been visited multiple times, and we still have so many places and things that we want to see and experience. We happen to be one of those couples who like spending all of our time together. We even worked well together when we did, so road trips where we get to be together 24/7 are particularly meaningful and enjoyable for us.

Evan is a talker, and I am more of the silent, "taking in all of the beauty around me" type. This is never more apparent than when we are in a vehicle together. I like to listen and sing to my music, and Evan likes to talk about all of the things that are on his mind, all ten thousand thoughts which he goes from one to another without completing the last one, on to another chapter, or even a different book entirely.

I try to keep up, correcting any mistakes that may come along (a habit that I am still trying to break), but I usually get lost in all of it. No matter, we are in vacation mode, not a care in the world except where to eat our next meal. Hotel accommodations are always planned ahead of time, much to Evan's chagrin, as I require reviews and assurances that the place is clean and without any bugs (the insect ones, the others I couldn't care less about), so we usually book before the trip even begins. Sometimes, we will decide, while on the road, where our next stop will be and then find a suitable place. Never do we spontaneously check into whatever hotel we find along the way. Expedia is one of the best inventions, ever, in my opinion for this reason.

We have road-tripped in quite a number of vehicles, most of them being agreeable, but a few were downright uncomfortable, requiring hot baths and Motrin to alleviate the consequential back pain. None was better than the Chrysler Grand Marquis, which we rented for two of our trips. It's a car with terrible gas mileage, but so comfortable that it makes a great road-tripping car.

Destinations that required flying were my least favorite. I hate going through security, especially after 9/11; even though I understand the restrictions and all, it is still a pain. I also dislike waiting in line to board and then waiting to exit. I always feel cramped and uncomfortable, can never sleep, even on a long flight, and hate when someone is behind me kicking the back of my seat, which always startles me. I have always had trouble with any type of travel, feeling nauseous and dizzy, and planes are no exception. When I smoked cigarettes, and we were no longer allowed to smoke on the plane or inside the airport at all, I would be especially miserable. Flying with Evan is pretty decent, though. He takes good care of me and doesn't get angry about my impatience. He really is an amazing travel companion.

Boats are off limits as I have had to endure several ferry crossings that didn't go well, so why even bother with a bigger one?

Whether we drive or fly, the purpose of all of our trips is to spend an extended amount of time together and experience new and fun things. The destinations are always secondary.

Early Pacific North by Northwest

October, 2004. Our first trip after our honeymoon was a quick week in Seattle to visit Evan's brother and family. I had never been to the Pacific Northwest, but Evan had been several times and loved it there. Ashley didn't remember much about it, although she had been there when she was younger. So we flew to SeaTac, and Aaron picked us up. We went straight to his home in Mukilteo, where Liane, Ethan, and Kyle greeted us. Their home was beautiful, warm, and inviting. The week was spent visiting different attractions around the city: The Space Needle, The Public Market where they throw whole salmon around for people to catch, The Underground Freeway system, Aaron and Liane's first home – a cute little green house that Evan loved, and just hanging out around the house. I loved all of the trees and the cool, clean air. Ashely had fun entertaining the boys and listening to old stories of her Dad growing up. She had probably heard these stories plenty of times, but I hadn't. It rained for a few days, but we didn't mind it at all.

After returning home, we never saw that house again. The next time we traveled to see them, they had relocated to Connecticut.

December, 2006. Our next trip to the PNW was to visit my best friends, Mel and Chuck, as they had moved to Suquamish, WA, the year before. For this trip, Ashley stayed at home with Janice and the pets, so Evan and I traveled to SeaTac once again. However, this time, we would have to take a ferry ride over to Bainbridge Island, where the small town of Suquamish is located. As I stated before, I don't do well on these ferry rides, so I had to spend the rest of the day recuperating while everyone else talked and had dinner. We hadn't really talked much since she moved away, so there was a lot to cover. We had tacos several times since they are Mel's favorite food, as well as some other Mel creations. She complained that they couldn't get decent Mexican food on the island, so she had to make her own all the time. We are VERY fortunate that we have several good authentic Mexican food restaurants in our little town in Washington. We also met a few of Mel and Chuck's friends who offered to take us on a tour of Downtown Seattle. So, we saw a few of the spots that we had seen on our previous trip, but this time, we actually went to the top of the Space Needle, looked at all of the shops and vendors at The Public Market, and just walked around downtown for several hours taking in the atmosphere and people watching. We were able to get a table at an upscale restaurant and really enjoyed the food and the company.

A short trip to see the rest of the island was enjoyed, and we even found a couple of properties that we considered purchasing. We tried the only Mexican restaurant on the island, and Mel had been correct in saying that it wasn't very good, but it was better than being hungry, not to mention that it is pretty difficult to really mess up a taco, just my opinion. The rest of our visit was spent playing games and sitting outside around the fire on their property, which was surrounded by beautiful evergreen trees. It was a great trip, and we would return again in 2008 for another week-long visit spent exploring more places and playing more games. These days, Mel and Chuck live in Queen Creek, Arizona, where it couldn't possibly be more opposite than the PNW.

Family Affair

July, 2005. "Hey, Babe, we should do a Colorado/Wyoming/Texas road trip so that I can meet the rest of your family." "That would be so fun! Are you sure that you want to spend that much time with my crazy family?" "Yes! This way, I can hear more stories about what you were like growing up, and we could go to Fort Morgan to see WHERE you grew up!" "Let's do it!" "Hey Ashley, would you want to go on a trip to meet Adda's family?" "Sure, Dad, but do we have to be gone very long? I don't want to miss the whole summer that I could be spending with my friends." "We won't be gone for more than ten days. What do you think?" "Sounds good, Dad."

We rented a Grand Marquis and headed to Cheyenne, Wyoming, where my sister Kim and her family lived. I hadn't been back to Cheyenne for a very long time, so I was looking forward to seeing it. I especially wanted to go and see The Trails End Trailer Park, where we had lived for a couple of years as kids. We all remembered being so happy there and at our school, Lincoln Elementary. I was doing so well there that I was supposed to skip the second grade and move on to the third grade. We moved to Fort Morgan before that happened, so I would go to the second grade at Sherman School in Fort Morgan. I was sad that we had to move and even more sad that I didn't know anyone on the first day of school. None of us girls, Kim, Barb, or Mom, had an easy transition. Dad thought that everything was fine because he bought us a larger mobile home to live in as well as a very nice place, Pagel's Trailer Park, to settle into. He did everything that he could to make us all happy, especially being able to come home after work every day.

When we lived in Cheyenne, he was over three hours away, so he couldn't always get home to be with us. Still, we all suffered from depression after the move, Mom especially, and we all handled things differently. My way was always to keep things to myself so as not to worry Mom about it. I gave myself a nice little stomach ulcer by the time I was fourteen. There were some good times, and I made some good friends while I lived there, but I was more than ready to leave it as soon as High School was over. I hadn't been back since 1995. Things had changed quite a bit.

Back to Cheyenne, Kim and Tim had just purchased a new home, and it was perfect for company: a pretty guest room upstairs, lower level with large couches for all of us to hang out. Barb was there, too. I hadn't seen her for several years so it was wonderful. Everyone loved Evan and Ashley, of course, and we had a great time hanging out. While Evan and Ash were on a little adventure, Kim, Barb, and I went to see all of the places that I had remembered and got to laugh and spend time catching up. Since we only had a few days at each location, it was hard to say goodbye.

We drove to Denver to see my sister Sherry and meet her new husband, Tate. Christina and her children were there as well, so all of us had a great time getting to know each other, especially Ashley and Christina. They bonded over those few days, and I always wondered how they would've been had they lived in closer proximity. There were a lot of tears when we left.

We headed to Fort Morgan to see all of the sights. All of my schools, the trailer that I grew up in, which was painted an awful purple color with the green mesh curtains still in the windows. I'm not kidding; my mom had purchased these curtains in this crazy gold color, and when she changed the furniture again years later, she dyed those curtains a dark olive green, and there they were. Even the green telephone pole that Dad had put in the middle of the yard was still there.

If I remember correctly, it was some kind of metal piping used on an oil rig, and it had footings for climbing. He painted it this ugly green color, and Mom was upset about it being such an eyesore. Dad promised to build her a little rock garden below it, and she could plant Morning Glories to climb up the pole. There was no one like my dad.

I took Evan and Ashley to where my favorite restaurant was while growing up. It was called La Paloma Mexican Food, but it was no longer there. Sadness. I would always get an enchilada and plain sopapillas with honey. Man, I can still remember how good it was!

We drove through Lover's Lane, over the Rainbow Bridge, and through Riverside Park, where we would go swimming and play on the giant swings as kids. Downtown didn't look the same, but it didn't look bad. It certainly hadn't taken the hits it did before ending up on the Home Town television show. The best thing about Fort Morgan, though, is that my best friend Marcia still lives there.

We didn't stay past late afternoon because we still had another destination to get to.

Midland Texas is brown, dry, and dusty; however, I have a sister and a brother who live there, and they had yet to meet my husband, so away we went, hitting some points of interest along the way, like Roswell New Mexico, a very fun place to spend an afternoon. I got me a couple of little aliens to bring home. I still have them somewhere.

Having a sister and brother in Texas came as a big surprise the summer of my senior year of high school. Dad had another heart attack, and Mom was told to get his affairs in order. As she was looking through Dad's papers, she found a number, thought it belonged to a family member, and called it. I am uncertain about all of the details, suffice it to say that she was able to reach my sister, Terry, who came to Colorado to see her father, whom she hadn't seen or heard from in over eighteen years! Dad was on a ventilator and couldn't speak, but what I heard Terry say planted a seed in my heart that would bloom into a full-fledged relationship with The Mighty Savior Jesus. I met my brother, too. His name is Larry. He hasn't been as forgiving of our father, who passed away just a few weeks later, but he has never borne any negative feelings about Tiff and me. On the contrary, I spent several weeks with him and his family before returning home to finish my senior year.

I went back, too, right after graduation, and I stayed with both of my siblings for a time, totaling almost nine months. Mom called me one day, asking when I was going to come home. This was the longest that I had ever been away from her, and I missed her terribly. I told her that I would come back and help her pack if she wanted to move to California, where her sister Susie and her brother Billy lived. She said yes, and we sold most of what we had and drove to California, a place where God didn't exist, according to Terry. I lived in The Inland Empire area of Southern California for almost forty years. Good thing I did; else, I wouldn't have met Evan, and who knows where I would have ended up.

When we got to Midland, it WAS hot and dry. We got lost, somehow (this was WAY before Siri guided GPS), so Evan called my niece, Priscilla, saying, "Somethin' ain't right" in a very bad southern accent, but we laughed over it. We finally made it to Larry and Gene's house, where we stayed for a few nights and enjoyed spending time with their grandkids, as well as meeting Samantha, Larry's daughter, for the first time as I hadn't been back to Texas for a very long time and this was actually the last time that we visited.

On our way home, we stopped in Bisbee, Tombstone, and Casa Grande. We were anxious to get home, though, and didn't make any more stops. We got to see some wicked thunder and lightning storms driving through Arizona – I haven't seen anything like it since. I love thunder and lightning and being home again.

New York New York Pt. 1

July, 2006. Aaron accepted a position with a brand-new corporation as its Chief Accounting Officer, which meant a move to the beautiful east coast town of Westport, Connecticut. Paul Newman and Joanne Woodward lived and raised their kids there. They would be close enough to Manhattan to go and explore whenever they fancied it. Just the history of this part of the country is so amazing that I was a bit jealous when I heard the news and then excited and grateful because Aaron asked if we could make a trip there and have Evan work on the home that they purchased and Ashley could help with keeping Ethan and Kyle entertained while Liane moved and unpacked their belongings. What I would do was unclear, but I could help Evan since I had already been working with him at his regular jobs in CA.

We sat down to plan. We all wanted to go to New York City for at least a few days and do the following: See a Broadway show, go to the Apple Store and FAO Schwarz, Statue of Liberty, Empire State Building (I wanted to see where Tom Hanks and Meg Ryan stood in the movie Sleepless in Seattle) Central Park, Little Italy, go shopping on 5th Avenue, stay in Times Square, go to Grand

Central Station, ride the subway, go to The Met, The Guggenheim Museum, lunch at Sardis, etc, etc.

We got an amazing deal on our plane fares, which Aaron paid for, as well as reservations at The Double Tree Hotel in Times Square, car rental, and BigRed Bus passes. I hated the seven-hour flight, got no rest at all, and was extremely tired when we got to Aaron and Liane's. It took me several days to feel better and be ready to work. The coffee was amazing, and no one can cook better than Liane, so we all ate very well while we worked. We all pitched in, and at least the first phase of the project was complete, so that the family could move from the small place they had been renting for the interim and into their new home.

After that we picked up the rental car and drove to Manhattan. It was HOT, record-breaking hot, as a matter of fact, and humid, so we were all feeling a bit out of sorts until the cool of the evening came, and we went on an entertaining nighttime tour of Brooklyn. The hotel was amazing! I had only stayed at one other place that was this nice on our engagement trip, so I loved the luxurious room and the giant tub in the bathroom. The moonlight shone into our window, and we could see that the city really DIDN'T ever sleep, with Times Square bustling with nightlife.

We were able to do many things that were on our list; we just ran out of time to go to the Guggenheim, and Sardi's was too crowded for us to go there for lunch. We saw The Producers (Matthew Broderick and Nathan Lane were long gone by this time), with Aaron and Liane joining us for the evening. It was definitely not appropriate for youngsters, but Ashley wasn't bothered by any of it. She had originally wanted to see "Chicago," but we had to say no to that one. One of the funny things that happened was our visit to The Metropolitan Museum of Art. Ashley spent the whole two hours in the Abstract Art section, and I wanted to be immersed in The Classics, so Evan stayed with me, primarily telling Ashley that he didn't like abstract art. The fact that he became an abstract artist is pretty ironic.

Evan also enjoyed driving in the city. He was competing with the cabbies over road space and the honking of horns. I wasn't worried about getting hurt in an accident. I was worried about Evan having to pay what it would cost if an accident occurred. No need to have worried; Evan proved, once again, that he could drive ANYWHERE and under any conditions.

The trip home was without incident, except, of course, my difficulties with any and all forms of travel. I had been to more places and seen more things in just three years of knowing Evan than all of my thirty-nine years prior. There truly isn't a dull moment being married to him.

Bucket List

June, 2007. I got a call from Mom saying that her only grandson, Travis, was going to be getting married at his Naval base in Florida and that she wanted to go. There were several different ways that this could play out-She could fly to Denver and meet Kim and Tim there, then they could all board another flight to Jacksonville. She could fly straight to Jacksonville, and Travis could pick her up at the airport. She could fly to Jacksonville, meet Kim and Tim at the airport, where they would rent a car, and meet Travis at a predetermined place. Last, but not least, Evan's idea was for the three of us to fly to Jacksonville, rent a car, and meet everyone at a predetermined place. We would also go on a little road trip, after the wedding festivities were complete, to some of the places that I had always wanted to visit, as well as take Mom to one of her bucket list places, New Orleans. Her reaction to this idea was to kiss her dear son-in-law on the cheek and hug us both. Mom had talked about going to New Orleans many times, desiring to go to Bourbon Street and party in all of the old jazz clubs, one by one. I was happy about this part of the trip as well. Having read books and seen movies that take place there, I had always wanted to see it.

I missed most of the first full day due to travel sickness and exhaustion. Evan woke up early and sat on the balcony of our room to watch the sunrise. He took a photo of it and later turned it into a painting that he titled Mayport Morning. It always hangs in our bedroom, where I can see it every day.

We all met for breakfast, and I had my first-ever sweet tea. I thought it was awful, but by the time we got back to California, I was a real fan and would make some from time to time, using the recipe that I got from a restaurant worker in Savanna, GA. When I received my hyperlipidemia diagnosis (excess fat in the blood), I had to stop drinking it and all other sweet drinks. I was sad.

After breakfast, we all got into two vehicles and headed south to visit Saint Augustine, the oldest city in the U.S., with its lighthouse and historical context. It was no wonder that one day wouldn't be enough to take it all in. We always said that we would go back there, but I have never been back to Florida, and even though Evan was in Fort Lauderdale for an art opening, he didn't get a chance to get back.

The wedding was the next day. We all got dressed up for the occasion. I had bought a new dress before we left. Evan looked amazing, as always.

We left the next day after renting a car that would take us to our next destination, Savannah! It was hot and humid, but I didn't care. I was in Savannah! There is so much history there, and I wanted to see everything. We only had a few days, though, so we would have to move fast. We did a lot of walking, eating, drinking (Sweet Tea), and driving around to different places. The Waterfront Walk and Forsyth Park were among my favorites.

We had dinner at The Godfather Restaurant; it had better have been some great Italian food with a name like that, and the next morning, Evan left early, alone. He came back a few hours later with some tickets for lunch at The Lady & Sons, Paula Deen's famous restaurant. Seems that people start lining up for lunch as early as 6:00 am, so they devised a system to give out tickets for the same number of seats they have in the restaurant. Everyone else would have to wait until the next day and get there earlier to ensure getting a ticket. My guy got there early enough to secure our seats, and so we stopped there on our way out of town. I had the crispy fried chicken with fried okra, baked mac and cheese, gooey butter cake, and some sweet tea to wash it all down. Also got myself a "County Cookin' Makes You Good Lookin" apron. Now that we were completely stuffed, we began the drive to the next destination, Atlanta, to see where Margaret Mitchell wrote Gone With The Wind, one of Mom's favorite novels.

Mom was also a great reader, and she's the one who got me started reading classic novels. I now have a pretty good library, and I add more all throughout the year. I especially love going to Powell's City of Books in Portland. Evan would find me a cart and then leave me there for hours, scouring through the blue room for favorite authors and their biographies. Most of my books are used.

We drove around Atlanta for a while and then headed to our next destination, New Orleans. We drove through an incredible rainstorm that caused zero visibility conditions. Cars and trucks were pulling off the road to wait it out. There was a poor guy on a motorcycle practically drowning out there. Once visibility was restored, I kept commenting on the giant ivy-covered trees along the highway that looked like monsters. I wish that I had taken some photos of them; they were truly creepy-looking. We also drove along the Mississippi River, and I dreamed of sitting with Mark

Twain and talking about all of the places he had been and written about.

We arrived in New Orleans, and before we checked into our respective Hotels (Mom stayed at a place that allowed smoking in the rooms, and Evan and I stayed at a place near downtown), we drove over to Bourbon Street, and Mom and I stood on the corner of Bourbon and Toulouse and we walked around a bit.

Mom wanted to start the evening at Pat O's, in the Courtyard, where she would order a Hurricane, a drink created by Pat, and got its name from the type of glass, a hurricane, that it is served in. She got the commemorative glass that you take with you, so we had dinner at Pat's and then followed Mom around as she entered an establishment, had a drink of some kind (or several), and then went on to the next place. We were practically accosted outside of Larry Flynt's Barely Legal Club and quickly crossed the street to get away from the action over there. This left Evan with a not-so-stellar opinion of Bourbon Street, but Mom wasn't bothered at all! We settled in one particular spot, where they had some of the original blues and jazz music that the city was famous for, until Mom was ready to go back to her hotel. It was past 1:00 am when we got to our hotel for the night. We had agreed to pick Mom up the next late afternoon for another round of fun on Bourbon Street. The next day Evan and I went out exploring the different quarters and found a street lined with antique shops and art galleries, so we spent several hours enjoying Royal Street, including a lunch buffet at The Court of Two Sisters where we tried some pretty strange things; turtle soup, bread pudding with whiskey sauce, crawfish, gumbo, shrimp etouffee, corn macque choux, just about everything, and sweet tea, of course. We saw a lot of the damaged areas that Hurricane Katrina caused, as well as Jackson Square with its large statue of Andrew Jackson and New Orleans City

Park. After a full day of exploring, it was time to pick up Mom for dinner.

At her hotel room, it was so full of smoke that I could hardly breathe. She had been watching forensic files all afternoon and never even went down to get the complimentary breakfast. She was ready to leave and hungry. We ate at Antoine's, the oldest restaurant in the city, and headed back to Bourbon Street for our last night. She thanked us over and over again for bringing her, but I think she was feeling a bit melancholy as she would like to have made this trip with my Aunt Susie, but we still had a great time, just the three of us.

The next morning, Evan and I decided to do a bit more exploring before we picked Mom up to go to the airport for our flight back to Jacksonville. We had planned to fly back home from here, but it was actually less expensive to rent the car to drive it back to Louisiana, then fly back to Jacksonville, and then fly home from there. Anyway, we went to a lighthouse and had lunch at Johnny's Po-Boys, a fried shrimp po-boy sandwich that we shared, picked up Mom, and headed to the airport. We had to fly in a smaller plane, which I didn't like, but it all went well.

We changed planes in Jacksonville, flew to Houston, had a three-hour layover due to a bad rainstorm, and finally flew home to Ontario Airport, where we found out that mine and Evan's luggage was loaded onto the wrong flight so we had to go back and pick them up a week later.

It was a phenomenal trip, and we have talked MANY times about going back, but we have yet to get to Chicago or Detroit, so a Midwest trip is in the planning stages.

Highway 1 Revisited

September, 2008. It had been over a year since we had done any traveling. Our lives were so busy that I was having a difficult time just getting through the days. We had been approached the year before to possibly take over the Junior High ministry, as well as our already thriving Young Adults Ministry. Evan really wanted to do it, but I was apprehensive about it, knowing how much work it is to run a junior high group and how time-consuming it is to develop relationships with the kids, as well as needed to have a large enough pool of volunteers to keep it going. I was also working part-time at my old job, IBF, as well as spending time with my mom on a regular basis. When we got into the truck after the meeting with Pastor Dane, Evan asked me what I thought, and I said NO, pretty emphatically, but he wanted to pray and fast and seek God's will on the matter.

We were now immersed in meetings, preparing lessons, studies, games for the kids, hanging out with kids after school and some weekends, etc, so a trip away from it all was very appealing. Ministry can be a two-edged sword, in that it is rewarding to do the work that God calls you to and wonderful to have the bonds that ministry brings but it can also be overwhelming for those of us who have trouble saying "no" to requests as well as trouble delegating. I wouldn't change anything for all of the world, though. I love all of my kids that I had in my numerous years of youth and young adult ministry. But I was tired and needed a break.

Our four-year wedding anniversary had come and gone, and we didn't do a lot for it since we had planned to take this trip down memory lane and visit all of our favorite places that we had seen on our honeymoon trip. One of our young adults, Danny, was going to be housesitting for us, so that was one thing that I didn't have to be stressed about.

We left on Monday morning, deciding to take HWY 5 all the way up to San Francisco and then take HWY 1 the rest of the way. We would go all the way up the coast, to Crescent City, and then into Oregon (First time for me), ending up in Coos Bay, where Ashley had been living for the past year. She had a boyfriend and wanted us to meet him.

In Frisco, we went down to Pier 39, had lunch, and shopped for a while before heading up toward Mendocino. We stopped at Point Arena Lighthouse for a photo.

As we were driving through town, we kept seeing signs along the road that said, "Studio Tour," so we stopped and asked someone about it, and for the whole week, different artists in the area were opening their home studios for anyone interested in seeing their artistic processes. We were very interested, so we stopped at a few houses, and then we saw a rather comical little sign for a tour, and so we turned onto this little road that led into a forest. We kept seeing signs, "Keep going, all is not lost," and "No, you're not there yet but keep going," "Don't lose heart, the promised land is just ahead". We were laughing at every turn, and when we finally reached the lady's home, we were delighted to find her in her studio, working, with her dog and cat companions looking on. She was a pastel artist, one of my favorite media, and she was really good at it. She gave us a tour of her work and the grounds. She gave me a postcard from a recent art show, and we headed back to the main road, with more of her signs leading the way out. Artists are interesting; most are either arrogant, peculiar, or introverted. This particular lady was peculiar, to be sure. Her name was Ann Kessler, and when I am asked what kind of artist I am, I say that I am of the peculiar kind. You can ask Evan where he fits on the spectrum.

We got to Mendocino and had a very late lunch before heading over to Point Cabrillo to walk along the lovely path to the water, then to our hotel, and finally back to the water to "watch Him take the sundown beyond the water's edge" Evan's words, not mine.

The next day, we went to Fort Bragg, and I wanted to ride The Skunk Train, an old steam-powered train that travels through the redwood forest, stopping in a place called Willits where one can get some refreshments, souvenirs, and take photos. The train then changes engines for the ride back to Fort Bragg. I loved the trip as we were in the open air, and it was just beautiful. Evan liked the trip to Willits but didn't like the fact that the view was exactly the same as the first trip, but he didn't complain about it. He will always do his best to take me on whatever adventures that I want to go on.

It was time to head to Ferndale, where we had spent part of our honeymoon and the horrible curvy Redwood Highway, a twenty-two-mile stretch that made me SICK! Evan was trying to take it slow in hopes that I wouldn't get dizzy, but it didn't matter. I told him to go as fast as he could while I had my face buried in a pillow and leaning against the passenger side door, moaning. Finally, in Ferndale, we checked into the Shaw House Inn and my favorite room, Betsy's Room, and we headed down to the window seat of the restaurant where we had our photo taken four years earlier.

We were sad to have to leave the next morning, but we had an agenda, so we headed to Crescent City, stopping for a quick fuel filling in Eureka, lunch, and a hidden lighthouse in Trinidad. In Crescent City, there are two lighthouses which we could barely see because the fog had rolled in. The waves were violently crashing, and the wind was howling so that I was completely bundled from head to toe. Evan, barefoot, climbed up on a rock so that he could get pictures of "the two lights dancing into the night."

The next morning, we would head to Oregon. What I always remember most about these trips is the beautiful tall redwoods and evergreen trees on one side and the ocean on the other with high cliffs and dangerous winding roads. Even though my vertigo wasn't as bad as it used to be, it still reared its ugly head just enough to wreck me during some parts of the trip. Evan noted that he did not get a welcome sign as we crossed the Oregon border and guessed that they didn't want anyone from California to come into their state. He also noticed that the speed limits were much lower in Oregon, which could explain the difference in traffic fatalities between the two states. We were meeting Ashley in Port Orford and then doing some sightseeing. It was wonderful to see her and to meet her beau, Mike. We toured the lighthouse and then headed to town for a tour of the Coast Guard Museum and a hike out to the grand cliffs. We drove to our hotel and watched the sun setting from the black sand beach. Our view was amazing, and I could hear the sound of the waves all night, my favorite sound to fall asleep to.

Evan woke up with a cold. His head hurt, and he looked done in. We had a long day of sightseeing ahead of us, so he showered and tried to make the best of it. We drove to Coos Bay and met Ashley at Safeway. She drove up in a little brown station wagon, looking adorable. She took us sightseeing around town; did I mention that it was wonderful to see her? We hadn't seen her for over a year as this was our first opportunity to take a trip up there. We had dinner and then played games at their place before retiring to our hotel. We stayed at The Red Lion in Coos Bay. It was really nice and reminded me of The Double Tree, with its wonderful pillows and crisp, clean linens.

I woke up excited because we were going to a botanical garden this afternoon, and I couldn't wait! I love gardens and flowers of all kinds. I also love fountains and ponds. It is called Shore Acres, and it didn't disappoint. There were greenhouses, ponds, plants that I had never seen before, and SO MANY flowers. I got a lovely knitted jacket from the gift shop that kept me warm for the remainder of the trip.

Our next destination was Reedsport, where we would visit with Evan's cousin, Della, and her family and attend their church. We LOVE going to church wherever we happen to be traveling. After lunch, we headed back to Coos Bay but made some stops along the way, another lighthouse (can you tell I really like lighthouses?) and a port with many sea lions lying about.

They kept calling out to us, Evan, saying that they wanted their photos taken, and I thought that the lady lions were flirting with him. Back in town, we met Ashley and Mike at an Italian restaurant, Evan's favorite, and right in the middle of dinner, Ashley excused herself, and so having our full attention, Mike asked Evan for permission to marry his daughter. We were both impressed, and we both thought that he was very responsible and respectful and that he truly loved Ashley. She returned before Evan had a chance to speak. I don't know any father who wouldn't want to have some time to think after such a declaration. The evening ended with Evan's "famous" root beer floats, made with DIET A & W, not regular, and vanilla bean ice cream, all of which he and I picked up at Safeway, giving us a chance to talk about the Ashley and Mike "thing." We both agreed that we felt good about them, so after our desert, Evan took Mike aside and gave him his blessing and support.

We left for the trip home the next morning. When we went out to the car, there was a note from the two of them on the windshield, thanking us for spending time with them. We were already missing them. I did have sort of an agenda for us to take a few detours on the way home to see some of the covered bridges in Oregon. Evan liked them as well; there was a story that went with each one, and I remembered reading a book about a man who was touring the country and photographing them.

I have to think for a minute. They made a movie about it with Clint Eastwood. "The Bridges of Madison County" Oh yeah, I read that book when it came out, but I hated the movie. I almost always hate movies made from books if I read the book first. Lots of times, I have wanted to read a book after seeing the movie first. Lots of classics, like "Random Harvest," "Gentleman's Agreement," "A Farewell to Arms," and even "Moby Dick," although I have yet to make it through the whole book. So, the covered bridge idea probably came from reading that book, and as I love going to places that I read about…my husband found a couple of them and took me to them. The Grave Creek Bridge is near Grant's Pass, and The Antelope Creek Bridge is near Medford. There are over fifty covered bridges in Oregon, and hopefully, we will get around to making a trip just to see all of them.

We raced down the 5 Freeway to get home. There isn't anything nice to say about the 5; there are no amazing redwoods or ocean views, just a brown, windy, desolate drive.

Go East, Young Man

October 29th, 2009. After only a short two-year period we handed the Junior High Ministry over to another couple but continued with the Young Adults. I was only sad to have to leave the kids. The workload for leading two ministries is handled well by some people but not by me. Frantic work environments also did not suit me. Now, we would be able to get back to a more "normal" existence and have time to breathe. A trip to the Youth Worker's Convention in Cincinnati had been planned months before, so we decided to go ahead and make the trip. Evan had another reason for supporting the trip. He had an art gallery in Chelsea, New York, approach him about showing in their gallery, SO we could attend the conference but afterward rent a car and drive to Chelsea to meet the gallery owner. This would also give me a chance to see some of the East Coast's historical places as well as stop by Alliance, OH, where I was born, and visit my mom's oldest dear friend Donna. Evan was looking forward to seeing the town from which I came, as well as asking Donna to tell some stories of what I was like when I was young.

I was not in a good place during this time. I was worn out and, unbeknownst to me, in a severe depression. I would wake up each morning and dread facing the day. I would later realize that having gone untreated or undiagnosed, this could have led to suicidal thoughts or worse. I wouldn't actually seek any medical help for this until the next Spring. I'm so glad that I did. I suffered needlessly for over a year, and I was greatly helped by medication and weekly counseling with one of my pastors. I wasn't physically up to the trip, either, but I put on my game face and tried to enjoy it as much as possible.

We flew to Hebron, Kentucky, and then took a shuttle to our hotel. We had the remaining part of the day and evening to rest before the conference began. We walked to a nearby restaurant and then took a stroll around downtown Cincinnati. It was a bit chilly, but such a beautiful night. Evan was having fun taking pictures with his new Nikon D5000. I was still using my iPhone camera as we didn't have the funds for both of us to have a fancy digital rig. (Later, I would purchase a Nikon, D3200, a camera that I still use today).

We woke up, showered, had breakfast, and headed over to the convention center for the first day of meetings and workshops. What I especially liked was the fact that all student levels were represented, so we had plenty of good information to take home concerning our wonderful young adults and the challenges that they were and would encounter. The next two days would be the same, with probably too much information to try to remember, but it was a good conference nonetheless.

It was now Monday, and Evan left early to walk around for the last time, so I slept in and was having my coffee when he got back. He loves to try to catch the sunrise no matter where we happen to be. I prefer sunsets, of course, especially at this particular time, as I am always glad for the end of the day so that I can rest and try to recuperate my mind and body. We had a quick breakfast and took a taxi to the car rental place near the airport, where we would be flying home. We planned to drive across Pennsylvania and on to New York, and then I wanted to go far north to Gloucester, Mass, as it has the oldest seaport in America. I love port towns, and I read a great book, "The Perfect Storm," written about the history of Gloucester as well as the great storm that took the lives of the men on a swordfish boat, The Andrea Gail, in 1991. (It was a good movie but difficult because half of it took place on The Andrea Gail during the storm, and there were no survivors to tell this part of the tale.)

We drove to Alliance and had lunch with Donna and her husband, Bill. We saw the hospital where I was born and drove around town for a while. After saying goodbye, we headed out on our long drive across Pennsylvania to New York, where we would meet Ruthie, owner of the Amsterdam Whitney Gallery.

Having already been to New York didn't curb the excitement of seeing it again. As we made our way to Amsterdam Whitney, we saw many other art galleries and could definitely see that the art district had changed locations as Soho used to be filled with an abundance but now only had a few artists' studios and galleries.

Right across the street, from Ruthie's gallery, there was a sign announcing David Hockney, so I got pretty excited since I love his work. It is simple but grand in size, so I insisted that we go there after our meeting with Ruthie.

Everything went well, and we both felt like this gallery invitation was legit and that Evan's work would receive a good amount of visitation. We headed across the street to see the Hockney show, which did not disappoint, and on to lunch at a little French bistro, and finally heading out of the city to make our way to Gloucester.

The drive to Gloucester was beautiful and the town wasn't as small as I had anticipated. I was so happy to spend the entire day there, visiting with local artists, seeing the Crow's Nest Bar (Mom would have LOVED this place!), and going to the museum and the port where the fishing boats deliver their huge swordfish catches. The evening brought more beauty and the sound of the sea from our sliding door. I was beginning to feel a little better both physically and emotionally.

Woke up feeling pretty good, and I was actually excited for the rest of the trip as we would drive south, along the coast, and it was a beautiful clear day. Massachusetts contains so much of our country's history that it is impossible to see everything in such a short trip. From Gloucester, we drove to Salem, where Arthur Miller's "The Crucible" took place, then to Boston, a remarkable place that we would like to spend a week touring, but we only had a few hours. I mainly wanted to have my picture taken at Harvard so that I could tell everyone, truthfully, that I went to Harvard.

We then drove to Plymouth to see the rock; it was small because of centuries of people taking a piece of the rock as a souvenir. It's protected now, so you can't actually touch it. (It is a bit disappointing maybe in the same way as going to a glass beach and finding out that there is no glass.)

We arrived in Sandwich, MA, to spend the night at an old bed and breakfast. We had breakfast with the owners, a nice older couple, before driving to Cape Cod. I wanted to go to Provincetown to see where the Mayflower landed and also all of the art galleries and history of the town. It took about an hour and a half to drive from Sandwich to P-Town, and it was cool to see all of the little vacation places that exist on this tiny little peninsula.

We saw Hyannis but didn't have time to stop there, so no John F. Kennedy Museum on this trip. I have always been fascinated by the Kennedy Family, so this was hard to let go. Evan isn't as interested in history as I am, so I had to make choices. Next time. Nantucket and Martha's Vineyard would have to wait as well.

P-Town was amazing, and the food, Oh Mylanta, was to die for. I loved the Cape Cod-style houses and the old street signs. We saw plenty of art and spent time admiring Cape Cod Bay. We bought shirts and a hat for me, then came the drive back across and to our next destination. New London, CT, is where my favorite playwright, Eugene O'Neill, spent his childhood summers at Monte Cristo Cottage. Another fascinating family, The O'Neil's… I loved the view of the beach from the front porch, and the path leading to the water. It was closed to tourists because it was off - season. I was sad.

Next we headed further south for the last part of the trip. We arrived in Westport, CT, to visit Aaron and Liane for a few days. We attended their church and got to meet Bob Fitts and his wife, Kathy; we were so blessed by their worship and love for Jesus. Evan also received a prophecy from Bob: He said that he saw Evan resting in grassy knolls and hearing God's direction through the soft, gentle breeze. Evan resting-not sure if that is possible, but he sure does hear from God and has faith like no other person that I know.

There was one more very important stop for us to make: Philadelphia! I had always wanted to go there, and you can probably guess why: The Philadelphia story took place there, as well as the filming of the movie Rocky. But there is so much more: Independence Hall, which was closed; The Liberty Bell, also closed, but you can see it just fine through the glass. At the Metropolitan Museum of Art, we just had to climb the steps and do a Rocky pose. It was a hard climb, and I had to stop several times before making it to the top and the Rocky statue was located just a few yards from there. By the time we made our way to Pat's for a famous Philly cheesesteak, the line was around the building, SO we went across the street to the other famous cheesesteak place, Geno's, and had a great sandwich, great for me because I didn't want cheese wiz on it, I wanted provolone. Evan wasn't satisfied with it and still wanted to go to Pat's.

Before heading over, we met another couple, who weren't really a couple as they had just met each other at a convention being held downtown. He was eating, but she wasn't. When we inquired as to why, she said that she didn't eat beef and wanted to find a place to get a chicken cheesesteak. Well, Evan, being the man who always wants to help people get what they want if it is in his power, offered to find a place that made them. Before we left, though, he wanted to get over to Pat's for a more authentic cheesesteak with the runny fake cheese. The couple waited in line with us, and then we went to the car, where Evan enjoyed his sandwich, and I looked on Google to find a chicken cheesesteak place. I found one and it was located in SOUTH Philly, in a not-so-safe neighborhood. Evan was not detoured, and we started to drive there with the help of the Maps GPS on the phone. Evan, always talking and looking at everything except the road, ran through a red light, which no one seemed to notice except for the ONE person in the vehicle who was actually watching the road. We got to the place, and indeed, this was a terrible area for us to be walking around in, but off we went to the small chicken cheesesteak restaurant, which had bulletproof glass protecting the workers and cash drawer. We encountered no problems, and the lady said that her chicken cheesesteak was worth all of the trouble. We dropped them off at their hotel and marveled at the fact that they agreed to get into a car with us as well as our inviting them to do so. Have I mentioned that with Evan, there is rarely a dull moment? We got to our hotel and finally went to bed. It was late, and we had a full day of exploring ahead of us. I woke up excited again because we were going to explore the Wissahickon Valley

Park in North Philly. It was a beautiful place where people bicycle and run as well as hike to the only covered bridge left in Philadelphia, The Thomas Mill Bridge. The hike to the bridge was about a mile long but pretty easy. The only problem that I had was that there wasn't a restroom on this route, and I had drunk several cups of coffee that morning. Having to "go" in nature is not something that I am comfortable doing, at all, but it was an emergency. We walked through the bridge and took a lot of photos of God's beautiful creation in all of its Fall glory.

It was time to drive back to Ohio and get to the airport. Along the way, we saw Valley Forge, Gettysburg, and Pittsburg, only stopping at Valley Forge for about an hour. We spent the night near the airport and flew home the next morning.

As with most of our trips, I was exhausted and needed about a week to recover from everything. We had looked at the Toyota Matrix as a possible future vehicle for us, but after this trip and having rented one, we decided against it; not a comfortable road trip vehicle at all. Of course, some of our other road trips involved expensive luxury vehicles, so we were a bit spoiled by this time.

It was time to get back to work and see what God would do next. Sometimes, we have taken roads that possibly weren't His leading, but He always did amazing things despite our presumptuousness. We would be flying back to New York soon enough for Evan's opening there—another chance for adventure in Manhattan.

The Art Of Art....Is Simplicity

January, 2010.

Evan's artwork arrived in New York, and we were at the airport to fly to JFK. Aaron picked us up and drove us into Manhattan and to our hotel. We decided not to rent a car on this trip, so we would be walking, taking the bus or the subway when we wanted to go sightseeing, very easy as we were in a good central location. I was still deeper into depression, but I tried to hide it as much as possible so as not to have Evan worrying about me when he should be enjoying this time. When we got to Amsterdam Whitney Gallery, we could see that Evan's display was separated from the rest, in a room Ruthie called The Ambassador's Room, which, if I remember correctly, was named so because her husband was a foreign ambassador.

It was perfectly lit, and his paintings looked amazing there. Evan spotted a damaged edge on one of the paintings, probably happening during shipment, so he found a shop that carried the faux products that he used for his art, so he took the subway over there and was able to repair the damage. I didn't do the subway this time; I was tired, and he was in a hurry, so it just made sense for me to stay behind. I used the time to relax and read.

That evening was the reception, and I had to try to keep my feeling of dread to myself. I didn't want to be around people at all, but as the artist's wife, there is that expectation to be there for support.

Aaron picked us up; he has been to all of Evan's important openings, and we met all of the other artists and their families at the reception. Ruthie looked hilarious in her ballroom gown and tiara, but it was part of the show. Evan was interviewed by a local newswoman who flirtatiously asked him questions, making him blush, and I stood in the distance watching. He was in his element. I felt horribly out of place and couldn't wait to go back to the hotel. Evan knew nothing of this as I tried to make conversation with people who approached me, and I DID enjoy seeing all of the art in the show. We were in no position to purchase art at this time, so I looked at everything cautiously. Whenever I fall in love with an art piece or artist, Evan always wants to find a way to get it for me. There were two particular times when this happened:

We were in Laguna Beach awaiting to hear about the jurying of his and other artists' work at The Artist Eye Gallery. We stayed just south of there, and on our evening walk, after dinner, we looked into the window of a gallery, and I saw the most amazing artwork that I had ever seen. The artist was Lillian Winkler. The painting was a nature scene, not abstract and not realism; it was something that I hadn't seen before. We checked the opening hours of the gallery and made a plan to go there the next day. The gallery owner wasn't very nice, but she did direct me to more of Lillian's work. I stopped in front of one of them, and I just started crying. It was so beautiful, almost magically inviting me into the art itself. There was a faint hidden path in the beyond, and I wanted to go there to see where it led. Evan saw my reaction and inquired about it. As she is a very well-known and established artist, her prices were in the $5,000 range, much more than we could spend on a piece, so I contacted Lillian and asked her if she was planning to make any prints available of that particular one, and she said that she was already considering it. She would get back to me with a price, and I guess my admiration led her to offer a print to me for much less than it was actually worth.

She signed it for me and added an inscription, *"To Adda, One Great Fan."* Oh, and the name of the painting is "Awakening." I got to meet her when I invited her to Evan's art reception at The

Artist Eye about a month later, as well as a few other times as she invited us to The Festival of Arts opening later that year, and we took her to lunch before we left for Washington. Good memories. The other time was in Cambria, CA, at the Seago Gallery. Sally Seago is an adorable woman whose artwork is cheerful and bright. I especially love her otter paintings, but this particular time, I heard Evan say, "Don't come back here," and you know what always happens in these cases? I HAD to go back to where he was, and I spotted it pretty quickly: a small framed painting very similar to the Lillian Winkler one, and I started crying. (I'm a little bummed right now as I'm writing this because her painting is still packed from the move, and I have no idea where it could be.)

Finally, back at the hotel, we talked about where we wanted to go the next day. There were some places that we hadn't had time to see on our last two trips, so we decided to have lunch at the Russian Tea Room, where we were terribly underdressed. The waiter said that we were fine, however, we had on expensive wool coats that we borrowed from friends, so he may have made a mistake there. We were seated near the back for obvious reasons, and as we were looking over the menu, a man dressed in very expensive-looking clothes came in through the kitchen and sat down at the furthest booth from the reception table, with a few associates joining him. Seriously, he looked like a mob boss, and we thought, "Yeah, it is New York, right?". We ordered our food, which I wasn't crazy about, paid our bill, grabbed those expensive wool coats, and got out of there.

There were quite a few art galleries in the area, so we made our way through them and then decided to go over to Carnegie Hall and see if there were any performances going on that day. There JUST HAPPENED to be one starting in about an hour, so we got to our seats in the nosebleed section. There isn't really any spot in this place that isn't marvelous, and we waited for the program to begin. It was a series of orchestral and vocal interpretations of Mozart's Requiem as well as other Masonic pieces. It was so beautiful and sad and glorious – an amazing experience that will not be forgotten. By this time, it was getting late, so we got back to the hotel, picked up takeout on the way, and spent the evening relaxing. We would be going home the next day. I dreaded the flight but was glad to get home to Pepper, Tucker, and Peanut. I would find and adopt Riley later that year, and it would be two years before we had time and the means to take another road trip.

Goonie Rocks

September, 2012.

We had discussed, on many occasions, our desire to return to Oregon and tour its coastal towns with their art galleries and fresh food eateries, so we plotted our course, not knowing that we would land in a little town that would capture our hearts.

Just before we left, some of our young adults had come by to see us off. One particular young lady asked if we would please make our way to Astoria and get her some "Goonie Rocks". Neither of us had ever heard of the place, but since we would be only a few miles from there, in Seaside, we would do her bidding.

Since we have seen Central and Northern California so many times, we raced up the 5 to get to Oregon as quickly as possible, with our first stop being Roseburg and stopping at a place called "Heaven on Earth" restaurant, which advertised chicken pot pie soup and other delectables. We had to stop and try it, and even though the restaurant was nothing to brag about, the food certainly was, and we were both more than happy with our meals. Our hotel in Roseburg was clean and comfortable, and I believe that I have mentioned before how important cleanliness is to me.

Evan is always raring to go early in the morning, and it takes a lot for him to allow me to be on vacation and not hurry to get on the road. He usually goes for a walk and loves to catch the sun rising. I love to wake up and have my coffee while I read or watch the news. Checkout was usually around eleven, and so as not to make him suffer too much, I try to be up and ready to leave by nine-thirty or ten.

If the town has a Starbucks, we will usually stop there to get Evan coffee and me some oatmeal if the free breakfast at the hotel doesn't suit me. We drove to the coast, stopping along the way to see different sights, one of which would give Evan a story to tell for years to come.

Evan pulled off of the road as there was a really pretty area with lots of flowers and a running stream. I got out to take some photos, and just as I was snapping one, the ground gave out from under me, and I went flying, upside down, legs straight up in the air, and fell into a thorny bush. Evan had looked up, and just as I was falling, he snapped a photo with my feet in the air and then came running toward me to make sure that I was alright. I was laughing, and so was he. I was unharmed, not even one stick from a thorn, and my back, which was easily injured, was fine. So, Evan got his photo, and mine was easily abandoned after my fall.

Our first coastal stop was Florence, an adorable little town that I fell in love with, as it has so many shops and these fascinating sea lion caves, as well as a great coastal vibe that resonates through its small town. Our actual destination was Lincoln City, where we would spend two nights and leave Sunday after church.

The best thing about Lincoln City was the art. There were several fine art galleries, and one, in particular, had an encaustic artist named Paula Blackwell. Like my other two favorite artists, she had an amazing piece that captured my heart, and like the other times, Evan purchased it for me. I see it every day as it is in one of my cubbies containing my vinyl record collection. We also visited the other galleries and had dinner at a great place called "Sharks Seafood Bar and Steamer Company." Wherever we go, we end up talking to people, sometimes locals and other times visitors like ourselves, usually asking more questions of them than the other way around. We have had a rich and eclectic variety of people come onto our path, and for each and every one of them, we try to be Jesus, showing unconditional love and acceptance to all.

Evan and I both love cheese, and knowing that the Tillamook Cheese Factory was only about an hour's drive from us, and since one of our friends told us to be sure to go there and get some "squeak" cheese, we wanted especially to experience that. Janice called us while en route and informed Evan that his father, Richard, had been born there. Evan thought that he had been born in California, so he was joking with me about lying on the marriage license that his father was born in CA, which made the document null and void so that, in fact, we were not legally married. I told him, "Nice try," and we had a good laugh about it. The factory tour was great, and we got to sample many types of cheese and ice cream. They made a special point to explain about the squeak cheese that it is part of the runoff of making other cheeses, and in fact, the curds are not aged but cut into bite sizes and sold as a snack immediately. They have a rubbery texture that causes them to squeak as they are chewed; thus, they are called squeak cheese. We purchased some blocks of cheese and other snacks to take back to the hotel for our dinner. It was Sunday, and we looked online to find a church to attend in Lincoln City.

We ended up at Faith Baptist Church, where we heard a new young pastor preach an eloquent message, and we were able to encourage him afterward. Evan would have left everything he knew in CA and moved there to be a part of this man's building of the church. We would have to wait quite a few years before we would actually be called to leave California. We would both be ready when the call came.

Along the coastline, there were many places to make a stop for photos and quaint shops. I especially loved Cannon Beach and Rockaway Beach, and I took some fun photos from both. There was a great deal of driftwood along the coast, and many pieces looked like animals of some kind. Evan never sees what I do, and he just shakes his head at me taking so many photos of them.

Funny photos aside, I did take some photos that I have used in numerous gallery shows, using different filter formulations to create something new and contemporary, as well as some great landscape photos that show God's beautiful creation.

I believe that I "came of age," so to speak, on this trip as far as photography was concerned. I discovered that I had a certain eye for seeing things. Evan pointed out that I saw many things in angles and preferred strong foregrounds in my photos. So true. If I look at my photography as a whole, I can see it everywhere. Thinking of oneself as an artist was also foreign to me. How could I possibly be an artist when I wasn't trained or schooled? How could he, having sold all over the country and many parts of the world, be an artist having been self-taught or Holy Spirit-led? While studying the Bible, I discovered that God called different people, by name, to build His Tabernacle: skilled laborers who were GOD-inspired and taught. This opened my eyes to new possibilities and gave me the confidence to begin investigating new ways to express my artistic side. Today, I love discovering new art forms and want to learn them all. I have made jewelry, junk journals, paintings, monoprints, and enhanced photos, my favorite being what I call Photographic Impressionism after my favorite painters Monet, Degas, Cezanne, and Renoir.

As I reminisce about my coming of age as an artist, it inspires me even more to keep exploring and finding new ways to glorify Him through whatever facet of art that He has me interested in at the time. Today, we have an opportunity to begin the gallery process again with a new gallery opening in one of my favorite places in Washington, Pacific Beach. We will both be showing there, and the owners are amazing in that they are happy to represent experienced artists as well as up-and-coming artists from this area. We owned and operated a gallery ourselves, so we know very well the inner workings and the struggle to bring the best possible art to the area. The fact that we began the artistic process together as a couple and that we are dedicated to continuing as a couple creates even more excitement and desire to produce better and better art for people to enjoy. We just purchased a shed so that we could have a studio in which to create. I would never have been able to pursue art, really, in any capacity, without my husband pursuing it as well. Singular pursuits tend to put distance in relationships, and neither of us wants that to happen in ours.

I was so happy to have my best friend Melanie meet us in Seaside for a few days of catching up as well as finding new adventures to inspire us. This was the first time that we would drive onto the actual beach, something that is still amazing to me even though we now live in an area where this is common. Mel was doing donuts on the beach in her Jeep and then allowed Evan some time to play as well. I sat in the Mini Cooper and watched. Donuts were not part of my diet and would not help my vertigo one bit. As we were walking along the promenade, Mel and I saw an advertisement at the very same time, and we both said, "HELICOPTER RIDES!" and, as usual, Evan would make it happen. I got to sit up front with the pilot, and it was AMAZING! The floorboard of the chopper was transparent, so our view was much enhanced. It was a great twenty-minute ride, and I didn't feel any kind of sickness during the flight. I would love to do that again someday; however, I have yet to go on a hot air balloon ride, and it's definitely on my bucket list.

179

We walked on the beach and hung out on our balcony at the hotel. It was cold, but we didn't care. I STILL had to have the sliding door partly open so I could hear the ocean all night. The next day, we popped into one of the art galleries to inquire about Evan possibly showing there. We said goodbye to Mel and headed up to Astoria, the northernmost city in Oregon.

I had never heard of Astoria, although I had seen The Goonies as well as Kindergarten Cop, but there obviously wasn't anything shown in the movies to really catch my attention the way that others had. The first wonderful thing that we saw as we approached was the Astoria-Megler Bridge. Now I know that I have mentioned that I love bridges, and this one is so unique. When I see it now, in person or in one of the many photos that I have taken of it, I get excited, just the same way I do when I see The Golden Gate or The George Washington Bridges.

The harbor, with all of the fishing vessels, is a scene that always moves me emotionally. It could be that I have read many books about seafaring or that life in a small community such as this appeals to me. The Columbia River is beautiful, and there is a great riverwalk through the town of Astoria. The food is fresh and fabulous, always an important aspect of any of our trips.

We still had another stop before heading back to Cali, so we didn't spend much time in town. We both loved the amazing craftsman and Victorian-style homes, and the downtown area had antique stores and art galleries that we could have spent the entire day looking through, but we were on a mission. Find the Goonie house and gather a few of the precious rocks, from the driveway, to take home for our girl Kristen. We found out where the house was, and we drove up the shared driveway, only looking at the home and not disturbing the owners who probably had no idea, when they agreed to allow the filming of the movie at their home, just how many people would seek them out and actually knock on their door, wanting a tour.

At the bottom of the driveway was some pea gravel, and Evan collected half a handful and placed it in a bag. We both fell in love with this little town and made plans right then to visit it again as soon as possible. We have made three trips to the area since.

Sadly, we had to leave in order to make it to Applegate Oregon in time to attend Jon Courson's mid-week bible study. Evan became a student of Courson, attending his mid-week study when he was at Calvary Chapel Costa Mesa for a time. We have used his commentary set MANY times while helping others to understand their bibles better. We really enjoyed being there, and since it was early enough in the year, the study was held in their amphitheater.

We spent the night in Medford and would make our way to McKinleyville, CA, where Ashely, now married to Mike, and their little boy Noah was now living. We were doing our best to keep to our traveling budget, so we took a chance on one of those blind deals on Priceline.

The way it worked is that you tell them your price range, and they find a place for you. We had booked this room for three nights, and when we got there, it was the absolute worst place we had ever been. It was so dirty and smelled bad, and you could tell that there hadn't been a single new thing added to this hotel for decades. Evan was pretty angry with himself and promised me that we would only have to spend this one night there. We checked into the Holiday Inn Express the next afternoon. It was hard not to be able to take showers after leaving that awful place, but we made it through the day and enjoyed being with Ashley and her family. The Holiday Inn is like The Double Tree in that every hotel is consistently good, so we were very happy to have a clean and updated room for the next two nights. We also traveled with a laptop or tablet so that we didn't have to rely on whatever television package was available. I usually choose movies that we have watched before or shows that are shorter in run time since Evan usually falls asleep before the end of programs.

We drove the nine hours home, talking about our favorite parts of the trip and how we wanted to return to Astoria as soon as possible. We presented Kristen with her goonie rocks, and you would have thought that they were diamonds with her reaction. We told her of how we fell in love with the area and had her to thank for the discovery.

These days, if we want to go to Astoria, it is a mere three-hour round trip instead of seventeen hours, each way, like before; however, when you are fortunate enough to live in the Pacific Northwest, the draw to go to those other cities isn't as strong. After almost three years of living here, we haven't gone to Astoria one time.

Are You Going to San Francisco?

In September 2013, we became busier than ever after we handed off our Young Adults Ministry to someone else in order to start a new Couples Ministry at Centerpoint. There was little time to take long road trips, so most of our vacations were shorter and closer to home. In the Spring of 2018, we decided to go to San Francisco for four nights, driving to our favorite places and FINALLY walking around Haight Ashbury, which I had wanted to do every time we were in the area, but either no one else was interested, or we didn't have time for it. There were people walking around, dressed in costumes, evidently trying to attract attention to keep the idea of it alive. There was none of the magic that made the area famous, no hippies walking about, no flowers in anyone's hair, just a place for weirdness and excess. I was about five when the hippie movement was going on, but I have always been fascinated by it. I was a bit disappointed but still glad that I got to be there. Evan tolerated it, as well as my going into different shops, looking around, buying a shirt and some pins; I like collecting pins and having them on my purses, backpacks, gym bags, etc. My favorites are rock 'n' roll bands, and smiley faces.

When Google Fails Miserably

Oregon was still on our minds, so we planned another trip, this time seeing some of the more inland places. We knew that we could encounter some snow and other winter things, but Evan could drive anywhere and in any conditions, so I wasn't concerned about it. In the planning stages, we were both looking for fun things to do, and we both love waterfalls, so we googled some different places like Klamath Falls. You would think with a name like Klamath Falls that there would be a waterfall, and when you google Klamath Falls a picture of a waterfall indeed comes up, but sadly, there is no waterfall in Klamath Falls. This debacle was on me.

Next up was The Dalles, also supposedly having a waterfall, Celilo Falls. It DOES have a very lovely view from up on the hill, where our hotel was located. It does not, however, have a waterfall. A series of dams built in the mid-1800s flooded the area. The Indian tribes used the area for their fishing as well as a place to do their trading among the different tribes and were compensated for its loss by the federal government. This one was on Evan.

Got Books?

My first visit to Powell's City of Books was on this trip, and Evan gave me five blissful hours to shop without complaining, sighing, or pacing back and forth. He actually wasn't even there, as he has no interest in books but loves to watch people, so he walked around downtown Portland and thoroughly enjoyed himself. We passed by a lovely park, so I had to stop for a photo. We love Portland, except for the traffic coming in and going out. It is a beautiful city filled with shops, cafés, and interesting people. These days, we just pass it by; even Powell's Books has not been visited in a few years. Sigh.

Northern Exposure, Twin Peaks, and the Flu

We visited Astoria and stayed for a night at a bed and breakfast, which had an amazing view of the city below. We did the river walk, ate at several of the local restaurants, and, this time, saw the Astoria Column, the Maritime Museum, and the Lewis and Clark National Park. The best thing about Astoria is the small-town feel and sense of community there. We then drove to Snoqualmie, WA, so that I could see the place where Twin Peaks had been filmed. We went into The Salish Lodge, which had lots of Twin Peaks memorabilia (in the series, the hotel was called The Great Northern). The waterfall was obscured by heavy fog, but we were told that if we went to the bottom of the fall, we might be able to see it. It was just okay, and I was a bit disappointed that we didn't get to see yet another waterfall. We DID see a few smaller ones on the way up to Astoria, nothing to write home, or in memoir about. Next up was Roslyn, WA, where the show Northern Exposure was filmed.

It was a bit cold and snowy, but we got to go to The Brick, the bar that the whole town of Cicely Alaska, hung out at, Rosyln's Cafe, where the moose mural is located, the Northwestern Mining Co. building that still has the Dr. Joel Fleischman handprinted letters on the front window with the Joel being misspelled and badly corrected. I bought a pink Northern Exposure Cap there, as it is now a gift shop.

We then drove to Port Angeles, WA, a simply gorgeous town with Victorian homes, breathtaking views of Olympic National Park, and so many walking trails and restaurants to enjoy. I was not enjoying much at this point because I had contracted some sort of cold. I couldn't stop coughing, and my head was killing me. When Evan got sick on one of our trips, he just kept going, but I was getting worse every hour. I could only muster up enough energy to take a few photos, and we had to get to our hotel so that I could rest.

The next morning, we headed to Port Townsend, another beautiful little town with historic buildings, a state park, and a lighthouse. I was too sick to enjoy it, though, and Evan decided that it was better to cut the trip short and get me home as soon as possible. He drove nineteen hours, only stopping to rest for about an hour until he got me home and into bed (no, not for THAT!) He really does take such great care of me all the time, but especially on trips. I can't imagine going anywhere of any significance without him.

A River Ran Through It

Spring 2019

It was just five months since Mom passed away, and my sisters had all wanted some of her things, but it was going to be pretty expensive to ship them. Evan had talked about wanting to take a longer road trip than the previous few years, so we decided to pack all of the stuff in the truck and road trip to Wyoming, with a few bucket list stops along the way. I had read the novel "A River Runs Through It" and I loved the tale of family and how much Norman loved fly fishing the Big Black Foot River. I saw the movie and REALLY wanted to go there after that as Robert Redford filmed it on location in Missoula, Montana. Evan has no interest in the book itself, but he loves seeing new places, and we both love any place that is centered around or near water. When we arrived, we were a bit saddened by the multitudes of taverns and breweries, but the town had a certain ruggedness about it, and we spent the better part of the first day just driving around the town. The Clark Fork River runs right through the town, so you see people taking their lunch breaks or having their dinner sitting by the river. We loved it.

The next day, we went to the local museum, and we both noticed a series of photographs on display there. They were all taken by a local photographer and bartender named Lee Nye in the back alley outside Eddie's Club, now Charlie B's. Each photo was a portrait of people of a time long passed: some beggars, some old-time railroad or lumber workers, transients, rail car drifters. These photos pull you in and make you wonder what the story was behind each individual portrait. Nye remained mostly unrecognized as an artist but not unappreciated by every visitor to Charlie B's establishment. I often think back to our time there and all of the faces staring back at me, daring me not to feel. We spent the rest of the day relaxing beside the Bitterroot River. It was a bit chilly outside, so we just stayed in the truck. Evan took a nap, and I just listened to the peaceful sounds of the river flowing and the rustling of the trees. The next morning, we chased some more of the rivers, ending at The Big Blackfoot and finding the Maclean cabin along the road, where Norman and his family would stay during their fishing expeditions.

Needless to say, Missoula did not disappoint, but it was time to get to our next destination, South Dakota. On the way there, Evan posted a live video on Facebook, letting everyone know that he would be doing several live paintings on this trip and would do a drawing to give the end result paintings away after we got back to California. His first live video would take place at the sight of one of my most desired places to see, Mount Rushmore.

It's a ten-hour drive from Missoula to Mt. Rushmore, but we took it slow, stopping to admire each larger city's Old Town: Butte, Great Falls, Billings, Gillette, and finally Rapid City. We were fifteen minutes too late to explore The Little Big Horn Memorial, I was pretty bummed about it. We spent the night in Rapid City and took the short drive to Mount Rushmore after breakfast. We stopped to check out the Borglum Story Museum, which has a really nice collection of works. The Mt. Rushmore Park is absolutely amazing and well worth the trip. Ken Burns made a great documentary about Borglum and everything that he went through in order to make his ultimate vision for the project come to fruition. I find that I appreciate historical monuments much more when I know some of the actual history behind them. We took some photos of the monument itself, walked The Presidential Trail, visited the Lincoln Borglum Museum, watched the film presentation, and looked over all of the displays. All in all, it took about six hours for us to see everything. The scale of the project cannot be fully appreciated without standing in front of it.

We looked around for a place to shoot Evan's first live painting video. Driving through the parking lot, we came upon a couple of Rocky Mountain goats that run wild through the park, so we stopped to watch them. Evan looked in his rearview, seeing a nice shady spot under some trees with The Presidents looking down in the background. Perfect!

During the live video, Evan talked about the fact that it was Good Friday and why it is a very special day for all Christ's followers. He also explained some of the techniques used to create his works of art.

It was a four-hour drive to Cheyenne, our next destination. By this time, Sherry had also moved there, so I would be able to see all three of my Midwest sisters at once. I was excited to give them the framed photo collages of Mom that I had made for all of us. A few years before Mom passed away, I took out a small policy to use for expenses. It was a blessing not to have to ask any other family members for money to cover costs, and I had some leftovers to do some special things for all of us. When Mom was going through a bad depression period, her doctor encouraged her to journal. We weren't able to locate all of her writings, but there was enough to put together a little book and have it printed for us. She wrote poems about all of her children as well as some of our friends through the years too. Most people didn't know that she was a writer. She didn't chase dreams of becoming anything other than a good wife, parent, and friend. Her sacrifice did not go unnoticed.

We arrived in the evening, so we visited for a short time before turning in. Evan planned to do another live painting and wanted to scout out some areas. I wanted to visit with Kim, so her husband Tim accompanied Evan, and they decided upon Vedauwoo National Park as the place for the next installment.

The Saturday after Jesus' death on the cross must have been a terrible day of uncertainty in the lives of His followers. Evan spoke about this, and his painting was a heartfelt depiction in abstract form. We spent the rest of the day visiting, and then we would be going to Barbara and Sherry's place the next day, Easter Sunday. Evan woke up very early and started driving further and further from civilization in order to find the perfect spot for his Easter Sunrise live painting. He sent me a text when he was ready, and I watched the sunrise on Facebook Live. He spoke about the Resurrection of Jesus and what it means for us today.

His painting was one of hope, the hope that we Christians have in that our physical death here, is not the end for us because Jesus rose from the dead, and we will rise as well to spend eternity with Him as His Bride. Easter just happens to be my very favorite day of the year and, for me, the best day in the history of all mankind. Jesus is my hope, and I know that I would not be alive today, had He not saved me and set me free from so many things. There is nothing more important than a relationship with Him. If you are not born again, you need to be! When Evan was finished, we all went over to Barb and Sherry's. I got to see all but one of my nieces and some of their children. I think one of them was sick because I woke up the next morning not feeling well. I would be under the weather for the remainder of the trip, but not nearly as bad as the Oregon Washington Trip. I was glad that we didn't have to alter our plans in any way, and as an added bonus, I got to see one of my oldest friends, Kris, when we stopped for coffee in Greeley, Colorado. We also drove by a property containing hundreds of Volkswagen cars and buses of all types. We really wanted to go up to the main house and ask to look around, but we had many miles to cross to get to our next destination.

Durango is an exquisitely beautiful little city in southern Colorado. We enjoyed just walking around town, taking in the clean air and God's amazing creation, but then we got to sample some of the FOOD! It's interesting how places become known for their culinary offerings, and this place lived up to the hype! Breakfast at a small cafe, light lunch, and then dinner, which we were very fortunate to have been able to get into the best restaurant in town, The Ore House! We laughed at the name but not at the food; it was some of the best that we have ever had, and we've had a lot. We walked back to our hotel, in food comas, and slept extremely well.

I had never been to the Grand Canyon, even though it is only a seven-hour drive from Grand Terrace, so I was raring to get on the road the next morning.

Being only a five-hour drive from Durango, we could take our time, enjoy breakfast in the cafe, and walk around the beautiful downtown. We got into a conversation with one of the waiters who asked if we had made the Telluride Loop, and not having heard of it, we were a bit sorry that we would not have time to do it on this trip. We wanted to see the sunset at the Grand Canyon, so we drove away, vowing to return to Durango and make that Telluride Loop. On our way to Arizona, Evan was caught in a speed trap and was given a speeding ticket. He was livid about it. He had been paying pretty close attention to his speed setting, too. I felt bad for him.

He HATES spending money on useless things like late charges and penalties. We got back on the road and made it to the Grand Canyon with plenty of time to spare in order to get cameras set up and Evan to get ready for his next live painting. As he was filming, a young couple approached him and asked if he was going to sell the painting that he was working on. It was a glorious rendering of the Grand Canyon, and as it was their anniversary, they wanted to have it as a souvenir. This was a difficult decision to make because it WAS a great painting and would fetch at least $500 at the Laguna Gallery. On the other hand, his heart went out to the couple because they really loved it. I took their phone number to let them know our decision.

In the end, we held on to that painting and hung it in the Laguna Gallery for $500. It was there for two months and did not sell. We could have looked at this situation in two ways: one was that I loved it so much and wanted to hang it in my own home, or two, it was meant to be given to the young couple. Evan asked if I still had their number. I did, and so I texted her and asked if they would still like to have it. The obvious answer was "YES," so I got their address, and we shipped it to them at no charge, knowing that it really was meant to be with them.

The sunset was magnificent. God's creation cannot be matched. As wonderful as Evan's painting was, no one can do what God can: the colors, formations, the fact that the sun rises and sets, and then the moon appears, the stars shining. Few places show the splendor of His creation like this place did.

Sedona, Arizona, is known to be a mecca for the arts, and so we were both excited to go there. The art district really is amazing, and they have everything: painting, sculpture, photography, glass, jewelry, printmaking, etching. Some of the styles didn't interest us, but I could have spent a fortune in those galleries. I have so much art that we have collected over our years together, and I don't have room to display it all. Many times, we will purchase just to bless the artists and encourage them. The food was good, too. We ate at a little southwestern place called Tamaliza Cafe. The portions were so large that I was intimidated. I often get that way because I know that Evan hates wasting money, so he feels like he has to eat everything of his and then finish mine, so I tend to overeat and then regret it terribly. I'm getting better about it, ordering smaller portions even though it isn't what I really would like to have, but saving myself from destruction.

Our friend Gary texted Evan and told him that we needed to go to Jerome, a little town high up in the hills with its old buildings and amazing view of the valley below, so we headed up there. It was a bit scary driving on those dangerous cliffside roads, especially because Evan likes to look at everything EXCEPT for the road. I was stressed out by the time we got there but quickly recovered because of the breathtaking beauty, old architecture, and tour of the Gold King Mine & Ghost Town. One of my favorite photos that I have ever taken was one of the La Victoria Glass Blowing Company; the crumbling remains of the building facade are one of the most photographed things in Jerome. I love the fact that you can see the rock formations in the deep background, and the sky was so beautiful that day.

We didn't do the tour of the glass company, but we could see them working behind the facade.

We DID tour the Chapel of The Holy Cross as well as Red Rock State Park when we returned to Sedona. Dinner was not worth mentioning, so back at our way overly-priced hotel, Evan started what would be his last live painting video for this trip. I always seem to get anxious to get home when I've been away for two weeks. I miss my animals most of all, somewhat like a parent could miss their children. We left the next morning for home, not even stopping to see Mel and Chuck; we had to get back to work.

We didn't realize, at the time, that the remainder of 2019 would have a seeming domino effect that would have us living in another state by the end of the next year. It all started after this trip, as I sat on my couch reading, in June of 2019. More about this, later.

Camping

After my first camping experience, it was a wonder that I ever tried it again. I am not the camping "type". I like my own bed, and I demand a clean bathroom and shower. Melanie had tried to get me camping for YEARS! I always used the excuse that it was all couples going, and since I wasn't married, I would be an odd man out. Not long after, Evan and I said, I Do, Mel wanted to know when we were going to go camping. I had no real excuse now, so I agreed to go camping in the fall of 2004. It was to be a Jeeping trip, which excluded me since I had vertigo, and I should have said no to this one, but I said that I would go, so we went. The campsite was dry and dusty, without trees or a proper restroom. What they brought was called the poop tent, a small tent with a bucket, a toilet seat, and kitty litter at the bottom. As with many other things that may not be comfortable for me or up to my standards, I tried to make the best of the situation.

I was there with Evan, Ashley, and some amazing friends, including Mike and Gina, and Patti (her husband, Chuck was not able to join us on this one.) and while they were all jeeping, I stayed under an umbrella reading. It wasn't as hot as it could have been, and I had very few issues. I DID refuse to use the poop tent and opted instead to use the facility in Mel and Chuck's motorhome. The evenings were nice, sitting around the fire, singing and laughing, playing whatever games we could come up with. The experience, as a whole, was a bit unpleasant for me, and I vowed never to camp again. A group of wonderful young adult students from our ministry would beg and plead for us to take them on a camping trip, and so I relented once again.

September, 2012. Our Young Adult Ministry was thriving, partly because we frequently had fun events to keep people interested and invested in the group. Like most groups, we had our regulars who showed up for everything, so when they begged for a camping trip, it was hard to say no to them. (I didn't know that we would only have them for one more year, as we would hand off yet another ministry in order to create a new one.) Evan contemplated locations and mentioned something about it to our neighbor, who was a Veteran and had access to Camp Pendleton's Beach, known as San Onofre. He could meet us down there to get us in, and we could camp right on the beach. Hmm, camping in the sand didn't appeal to me much, but I do love the ocean, so how bad could it be? The kids were so excited, and we were even able to talk our worship leader, Ben, into coming along. We left Friday afternoon, stopping at In n Out on our way out of town. It was an almost three-hour drive to San Diego, with traffic, so we arrived early evening to set up tents and get a fire going. We spent some time worshipping Jesus, and then Evan gave us a bible lesson. I was tired, though, and wanted to go to bed.

Evan, being preoccupied quite often from having three careers, forgot to bring our air mattresses and sleeping bags. We used the extra sleeping bags that we brought from the high school ministry and tried to make the best of it, but when you try to sleep on sand, it's hard! Sand is just crushed rock, so a sleeping bag may be enough for the youngsters, but we were both miserable and would probably get no sleep at all.

Evan decided to go to the local 24-hour Walmart and get us supplies. He came back with two air mattresses, sleeping bags, and pillows, so we were able to rest comfortably and sleep. There was plenty of junk food for breakfast, and Evan got me a coffee so I could survive the morning. Let me tell you, I get extremely grumpy when I don't have my coffee right when I wake up. This is why I have always made the coffee, the night before, to be able to turn it on as soon as I wake up or have one of the programable ones so that it is already brewed when I get out of bed. Evan has learned over the past nineteen years how important my coffee is to me. It really isn't about caffeine but the hot, freshly brewed taste and smell of it. Unfortunately, I lost my sense of smell and taste when I had Covid 19, so I can no longer smell it, but I still have it first thing just the same. Saturday was filled with fun and games, reading for me, and the kids swimming in the ocean. I don't swim in the ocean. The one and only time that I did, my whole body broke out into a painful rash that took a week to heal.

Needless to say, I never swam in the ocean again. I won't even get my feet wet in it. When Evan and I walk on the beach, he walks on the ocean side, enjoying the refreshing coldness of the water while I keep my shoes on, many times opting for rain boots instead of regular shoes when beaching.

We had another large fire that evening and what we called "church on the beach." Any opportunity to sing with other believers and hear the Word of God is a blessing for me. We slept well. I loved that I got to hear the "real" ocean waves as I was falling asleep instead of the ocean waves and rain CDs that I had used for years to help me cope with the tinnitus that I have. This would be the number one factor in my agreeing to go and even wanting to go camping in the future. Sunday morning, we had breakfast, cleaned, and packed up to go home. I considered this to be my inaugural beach trip, and I completely enjoyed it.

September, 2014. We didn't have the time to go camping for a full two years after the last one. Evan had spoken several times of his going to Doheny State Beach when he was growing up, so one of the times that we were in Laguna, we drove a bit further south to Dana Point to check it out. We both loved the close proximity to the beach that the campsites had, and we found a site that we agreed was perfect: Site #90. It wasn't right on the beach, but you could still hear the ocean, and the restrooms were only a few steps away. It is important because we both like to drink hot tea or decaf coffee when we camp but have to use the facilities at least once in the middle of the night. The things one has to think about as they get older. We made our reservation and couldn't wait to go on our very first camping trip, just the two of us. There are plenty of bike paths at the park, so we brought our bikes and enjoyed riding in the cool of the evening. We rode a bit further out on the second day, and Evan decided to ride up a steep grade of the parking lot, so I did the same; however, I was not able to get off the bike quick enough to get my feet on the ground, and I fell sideways, just missing hitting my head on a rock, and cut up my leg pretty badly. Evan felt terrible, but it was my fault. I'm terrible on a bike, and I shouldn't have attempted it.

We patched me up, and I was sore but alright.

It was a bit too warm for a fire, but we had one anyway. When we are both relaxed and away from home, we sleep so well. I'm sure that the drop-in temperature plays a role as well. Some people have to be warm and cozy at night, but I prefer to be cool but not cold. We didn't have trouble with people being too loud, either. Had I not had the fall, this would have been a perfect trip. We would plan a much more ambitious experience for the next one.

May, 2015. Big Sur is a gorgeous place in central California, and one of its state parks, Julia Pfeiffer Burns, is its most beautiful campground. The Big Sur River runs right through the park, and the nature hikes are breathtaking. The other great thing about this park is NO CELL SERVICE! This was our first unplugged trip ever, so we wouldn't be tempted to take phone calls or spend time cybersurfing.

I took books, lots of books to keep me occupied and relaxed. Evan made fire constantly. He brought his ax and lots of firewood, so it was going all the time. We spent the first two days just resting and taking walks around the park. The next few days were for exploring, and we left campus to go to nearby sites like Pfeiffer Beach, with its main attraction, Keyhole Rock, which has a magnificent natural arch that pulses with seawater and sunlight. When the sun is setting, you can see it right through the arch, and it is just magnificent. It was extremely windy, so the umbrella was useless, but we got there after the sun had already begun to set, so I was alright, just cold. Day four was spent hiking at Point Lobos, and then the popular Waterfall Overlook Trail, which doesn't sound too difficult, being only a half mile long, but the whole trail is uphill and very rocky. I was wearing rain boots, and my feet were getting sore from stepping on all of the rocks. No way would I have gone had I known how difficult it would be, and the promised waterfall wasn't at all worth the trouble.

We ate at the local restaurant and spent a little time in the Henry Miller Memorial Library. I was tired from all of the day's activities, so I was glad to get back to our campsite to relax. Day five was spent riding our bikes and exploring the rest of the campground. This had been our favorite camping trip thus far and one that we talked about doing again. We never did, but we found some other good places to camp that were closer to home.

January, 2017. We drove to South Carlsbad State Beach Campground during another one of our trips to Laguna. Some friends of ours had spoken of it, and we decided to check it out.

The campground sits up on a ledge, looking down on the ocean and beach. We made a reservation to stay there during our end-of-year vacation instead of going on a long road trip. We both brought art supplies, and I brought books, of course, and we would go into the nearby towns to explore them, pick up more supplies, or go to one of the restaurants or cafes. We brought plenty of food with us, but we like eating at restaurants, so we had at least one meal every day at one of them. There was also a vintage theater, The La Paloma, nearby, and I wanted to go.

They were playing Manchester by the Sea and the title, being about the sea, interested me a great deal. Didn't know what it was about, but we bought the tickets and spent some time looking around the theater before the movie started. It was not a funny or action-packed movie but a sad and tragic one. Poor Evan. He DID say that it was well done, and the acting was phenomenal. I loved it and have watched it several more times. It's not for everyone and certainly not church-appropriate, but it won several Oscars, and just the scenery alone is worth the watch.

Now that I had my movie and popcorn fix, we went back to the campsite, and it was raining. Our tent was waterproof, so we boiled water for our hot tea and played Phase Ten until it was time to sleep. By this time, I had gone into Menopause, so I began to have a lot of trouble with the sleeping bag being too warm and my temperature blazing even though it was in the 40s outside. It would take me an hour, most nights now, to actually get fully into the bag and able to sleep. I had to have a fan on all the time, and Evan had purchased a solar-powered Yeti to take on trips so that he could still use his C-Pap machine at night, so I just plugged into there and had a fan right in my face all night long. I still, to this day, have to have a fan on my face at night. Oh, the perils of getting older. The next day, I rode my bike, and Evan worked on some small paintings. It just amazes me how he can make the colors on the painting look exactly like the scene he is painting.

One of the problems with Evan being an excellent artist is that I always want to keep everything. I still have two of the paintings that he did that week in South Carlsbad. Of course, they are packed, and I have no idea where they are right now. Going home after an amazing time away is hard. We both get a little melancholic and have trouble getting back into the rhythm of things. If we were independently wealthy, we would probably travel all of the time, only stopping back home to reconnect with our friends and church. We are not, however, and so we must return to the grind like most other people. We would camp at South Carlsbad again in the Summer of 2017 and Spring of 2018. We miss going there, and hopefully, we will be able to take our RV and glamp at the campsite on the top of the hill on a future trip.

Adventures WITHOUT Babysitting

Living in Southern California has its drawbacks: traffic, overcrowding, long waits, high crime, traffic, faster pace of life, traffic. You get the picture, but Southern California also has its perks, and one of them is the ability to take a wide variety of day trips. The possibilities are pretty endless when you can travel just an hour or so from home and have major attractions, beaches, art galleries, lots and lots of food choices, museums, nature walks, sporting events, etc. We would try to go on at least one good day trip every few months. Evan always likes to take me to a new place on my birthdays. He took me for my first trips to Sea World, Knott's Berry Farm, and The Aquarium of the Pacific.

He also likes to be secretive about where we're going. I would ask lots of questions because depending on where we were going, I would need to know what to bring, what to wear, will it be cold, will I have access to food, or if we should bring some. I don't like guessing games or not being in the know, and I really don't like surprises. None of his surprises have been bad, but I would always just feel better if I knew what I was getting into. For our trip to Knott's, I asked him what I should wear. He said that it didn't matter, so I decided to wear overalls, specifically the ones that my friend Lissa had sewn with all kinds of Snoopy material. He said that my choice was perfect, but I still didn't have a clue. When we exited the freeway, there was a sign that pointed to Knotts Berry Farm, so I finally figured it out since it was right in front of me. We've been on literally hundreds of day trips, but a few stand out.

Food

We have been fortunate to have the ability to travel for no other reason than to satisfy our culinary desires over the years. Evan loves to eat at fine dining restaurants, and I like eating, so it works out pretty well for us. He finds driving to be relaxing, and I like to sit and enjoy the scenery and sing while he drives. If someone tells us of a great dining experience, we always want to go and try it for ourselves. We drove to San Diego one day just to eat at George's at the Cove. What that chef can do with a pork chop!

We discovered South of Nicks in San Clemente just because the other restaurants were too packed out, and we needed to eat quickly and get to one of Evan's art shows. We couldn't wait to go again to enjoy their salmon tacos and poached sea bass. A few months later, they opened another restaurant in Laguna Beach, and since we had to be there a few times a month, we would visit there regularly. Two other Laguna favorites, The Sapphire and K'YA, are both just steps from The Artist Eye Gallery, where Evan was a resident artist for nine years. For fish, we like Market Broiler and The Crab Cooker.

Here in Washington, we have found new favorites like Jean-Pierre's Three16, Rediviva, Beau Legs, Victor Tavern, La Spiaggia Ristorante, Wild Irish Pub (best burger EVER), Al Carbon Steakhouse, Samurai Sushi, and so many more. Only two of the aforementioned are located in Aberdeen. For the rest, we had to drive about an hour to Olympia or as far as Seattle.

We always stop at The Victor Tavern in downtown Seattle whenever we see a show across the street at Jazz Alley, which is probably our favorite day trip right now. We have seen seven shows so far, with my favorites being Chris Botti and David

Sanborn—Evan's favorite featured Rick Braun & Richard Elliot in a joint program that was very entertaining.

The funny thing about jazz and Adda is when I worked at Video Mart in San Bernardino, CA, the owner, David, would play his favorite modern jazz CDs, and it would drive me CRAZY! I hated the ten-minute long riffs and non-melodic arrangements so much that I even stopped listening to Miles Davis and other much preferred smooth jazz artists for quite a while. I'm old school with my Rock n Roll, Country, and Jazz. I like very little of the music that happened after the 1970's. I was reunited with jazz, years later, when I heard an old tune by Jimmy Smith, "I'll Close My Eyes," in a movie. I've even got Evan listening to it.

Back to the food. Evan doesn't really like the food at Jazz Alley and would rather not eat there, but I think that their prime rib is really good, and as long as they have mashed or baked potatoes available, I usually order that. Evan prefers Italian, BBQ, and good burgers. I like rib-eye steaks, prime rib, and baked potatoes. We both like fish, but Evan doesn't like "fishy" fish like trout and catfish. I love salmon, cooked about any way, and Evan loves sea bass. We have tacos, whether at a restaurant or cooked at home, at least once a week. I still love going to Taco Bell for a Mexican Pizza and those little cinnamon twists.

I laugh when I think about how many trips we have made over the years just to have the food that we were craving at any given moment. We don't watch Throw Downs with Bobbly Flay anymore because it's just too hard to find lasagna or fish tacos at ten o'clock at night.

Abandoned

In 2011, I watched a documentary called "Abandoned in America," and I got hooked. I have always loved old, dilapidated buildings, but now that I know there are entire CITIES filled with them, it created an obsession, and with one of the features, The Salton Sea, so close to home, I would pester Evan to take me there for years. While on a gallery scouting trip to Palm Springs, he could deny me no longer.

Located near Brawley, The Salton Sea was a man-made disaster created in the early 1900s when water from the Colorado River floodwater breached an irrigation canal being constructed in the Imperial Valley and flowed into the Salton Sink, destroying the town of Salton, creating a lake body. Birds and other wildlife began migrating there, and the lake was stocked with different species of fish. "As the fish began to thrive, it fueled a recreation boom in the 1950s, and the inland desert sea became an inviting sport-fishing and vacation destination. Its coastline developed numerous resorts and marinas catering to water skiers, boaters, and fishermen. Billed as "Palm Springs-by-the-Sea," restaurants, shops, and nightclubs also sprang up along the shores. The lake enjoyed immense popularity, especially among the rich and famous, as movie stars and recording artists flocked to the area. From Dean Martin to Jerry Lewis, Frank Sinatra, and the Beach Boys, the lake became a speedboat playground." (Ref. legendsofamerica.com)

It took several hours to explore just the perimeter, and I wanted to get out and look around as well. The smell is absolutely horrible because as time has passed and having no outlet, the water has become more and more saline, killing the fish. What appears to be white sand is actually crushed fish bones and salt. You get used to the smell, and many people camp at the still-open campground. I wanted to camp there, but Evan said no. He doesn't say no very often, but as I could forgive the smell and general yuckiness of it all, Evan was sickened by it. I took some photos, but as it wasn't time for the sun to set, I didn't get "the money shot" that always comes up when you google The Salton Sea. It was a great experience, though, and my favorite thing was a cool sign from the Ski Inn at Bombay Beach with the abandoned mobile homes beyond.

Excuse Me While I Touch the Sky

At the beginning of the bungee jumping craze, I decided to experience it for myself, so I made plans to go with two of my co-workers. Mom threw a FIT and would not stop begging me to reconsider, her best reason being that if I became paralyzed because of it, she didn't want to be the one to take care of me for the rest of my life. She made me promise never to go bungee jumping, and so I watched as my co-workers jumped and felt the thrill of falling without the injuries that would certainly occur if not being attached to a long springy chord. Some twenty years later, a friend texted me a Groupon ad for a skydiving package. "Wanna Go?" she asked. I showed it to Evan, and he told me that we should call her bluff. So I messaged back, "Sure, when?" Now, my promise to Mom was that I would never bungee jump. She never said anything about skydiving!

Groupons purchased, date set, no mention, whatsoever, to Mom, we headed to Oceanside, CA, where we would go through a training period and then board a perfectly good airplane that we would jump out of. When you're a novice, you have to jump tied to a professional who will encourage you when it comes to jumping as well as pull the chord on the parachute. I met my jumping partner, a kid named Nick, who jumped with his flip-flops rubber-banded to his feet, and he assured me that he had years of experience and that he wanted me to land on my feet, not my rear end. "Just follow my lead, and we will have a great landing." I'm still a bit puzzled that I experienced no fear at all. My only concern was how I would feel afterward. I was the first to go from our party, and as we made our way to the door, Nick told me to jump forward and out, not down. Off we went, and it felt more like floating than falling. The air was cold, and what I noticed most was that my mouth was dry.

I didn't want any spinning or other tricks as I would really rather not vomit and ruin the whole experience. We touched down for a smooth on-our-feet landing. My elation didn't last very long, as I got extremely dizzy and nauseous as soon as we boarded the shuttle back to headquarters. The experience was worth the consequences, and I would actually go a second time with Evan and Britt a few years later.

Sports

Anyone who knows me knows that I love sports and can intelligently watch just about any of them. When I was ten years old, my grandpa moved to Fort Morgan and into Pagel's Trailer Park. Grandpa watched sports all the time. Whatever the season offered, he was watching. I loved Grandpa, and I would go to his place on Saturdays and Sundays just to spend time. While we visited I would also watch sports with him. My earliest memories being of the World Wrestling Federation and my favorite star, The Cusher. I thought it was real, and it would be some time before I was either told that it was acting or I figured it out on my own. With that knowledge, I ceased being interested in it but there was always something to watch at Grandpa's.

Saturdays had ABC's Wide World of Sports, and I can still remember the opening with the poor guy on the skis wiping out. We watched the whole program, with bowling being our favorite. In the Spring, we watched baseball, my favorite teams being the Cincinnati Reds and Philadelphia Phillies. I had favorite players, too, Pete Rose with his head first slide and Mike Schmidt because he was cute. The Reds won back-to-back World Series in '75 and '76. It was pretty amazing for my first two years of fandom. I remained a fan as long as I watched baseball. Basketball started after baseball ended, so that was convenient. Grandpa liked The Celtics, so I liked them too. Larry Bird was my favorite player, and like the Reds, the Celtics won two titles that decade. Eventually, I became a Lakers fan and remained one as long as I watched basketball. Hockey is a favorite because I like the pace of it and the fights. Grandpa liked The Pittsburgh Penguins, and I liked penguins, so it was a good fit. They weren't a very successful team, and we didn't get to see many of their games. I eventually became a Kings fan, especially after attending two Stanley Cup Playoff games as a novice photographer and film runner. The Penguins did become a powerhouse during the 1990s and have won five Cups since then. Tennis was really great in the 1970s, and we watched all of the grand slams. Jimmy Conners dominated, but John McEnroe was the most entertaining. I also liked that they always showed the fans, many of them athletes from other sports or movie and television stars. When I started watching Boxing, George Foreman was the Heavyweight Champion, but in October of 1974, he was beaten by Muhammad Ali in what was called "The Rumble in the Jungle" because it was fought in Zaire. All of the big boxing matches were announced by Howard Cosell and broadcast on ABC. Grandpa hated Cosell, but I thought he was funny.

I continued to watch boxing until it went to pay-per-view. I thought that Mike Tyson had the potential to be the greatest heavyweight of all time, but he left his original manager and Don King became his manager and promoter. Unfortunately, the young boxer was overtaken by the limelight and constant distractions and ended up spiraling down. His interviews are always entertaining, though.

I love watching the Summer and Winter Olympic Games. I just wish that they came around every two years instead of every four. My favorite summer events are Swimming, Diving, Water Polo, Cycling, Table Tennis, Badminton, and Ladies Gymnastics. In the Winter Olympics, I like Ski Jumping, Ice Racing, Singles and Couples Figure Skating, Bobsled, Luge, Curling, Giant Slalom, and The Biathlon. The DVR revolution has changed and improved sports watching to such a degree that I can hardly remember what it was like only to have one channel to watch them on. I set the DVR for all of my favorites and spend many hours binge-watching and fast-forwarding the commercials. Olympic coverage can make you crazy, though, as they spend less time showing the sport and more time on the drama stuff.

When I got married to Evan, we decided that we would only have time to focus on two sports, one of my liking and one of his. My choice was and will always be football. I love football more than almost anything. I'm extremely sad during the off season and spend way too much time watching when the season begins. It doesn't hurt that there are multiple games during the day on Sunday, one on Sunday night, one on Monday night, and another on Thursday night. I started watching with Grandpa, and his team was the Pittsburgh Steelers. We would see them win four Super Bowl titles in the '70s, and I remained a Steelers fan until the last of the Dynasty players retired, and I decided I would quit watching football forever. Mom ended up becoming a Denver Broncos fan and begged me to watch with her, so I became one, too. I grew up some, so I don't let go of my team just because key players retire or we lose five Super Bowls before winning one.

The Broncos have three now, and that is more than many other teams who have yet to win one or, if they are fortunate, more than one. Evan likes football, but not as much as I do. He roots for the Broncos but gets really mad when they play poorly. For example, when we lost so badly in the Super Bowl against the Seahawks, he threw his Peyton Manning jersey in the trash. Thankfully, I saw it before he took the trash out and retrieved it. He was glad that I did, but that just goes to show you that some people get a little more wrapped up in things than others. Mom always watched every game until the end, no matter how badly we were losing. I get disgusted and leave or do something else to distract me from a losing game, but I don't throw my jersey or hat into the trash.

Evan had to choose a sport to watch, too. It was only fair. He likes soccer a lot, but mainly when the World Cup happens, and that only happens every four years, so he chose golf. He likes to play golf and watched a lot of it when he was in his twenties. His favorite players were Tiger Wood and Phil Mickelson. I like to watch golf as well. I started watching with Grandpa during one of golf's best decades. Jack Nicklaus was my favorite, but I also liked Tom Watson and, later on, Hal Sutton. I lapsed a bit in my golf viewing for a time, but when Tiger came onto the scene, my interest was renewed. I was also a fan of Phil, so we were pretty even on this one.

We follow lots of other players these days. Adam Scott, Jordan Spieth, Bubba Watson, and Scottie Scheffler are a few of my favorites. We have also attended the opening day of a few tournaments, like the Farmers' Insurance Open in Torrey Pines and The Genesis Open at The Riviera Country Club in Los Angeles. That was the best one because almost all of my favorites were there, and I got to talk to Angie Watson, Bubba's wife, and meet Terry Gannon, one of my all-time sports heroes. Terry had played for NC State in the 1983 NCAA Division One Men's Basketball Championship, (a tournament that I remember watching) as well as being a sports broadcaster, (a career that I seriously considered pursuing). I saw the documentary, "Survive and Advance," which featured Terry and some of the other players and coaches from that Championship team. I recognized Terry from his coverage of the Olympic Games as well as being one of the commentators on Golf Network. We headed to the press box at the end of the tournament and waited for him to come out. He was a little surprised that I wanted to meet him and not the many golf stars signing autographs nearby. Evan took our photo.

There was a new golf league established a few years ago called LIV Golf. Some of our favorite players decided to move to that league and play in tournaments that were for individual glory but also the chance to be part of and win as a team. Many people have been very negative about it, but we like it and don't care what other people think of it. It is really just another chance to watch a sporting event, which makes me happy. I love these Hunter

Thompson quotes about my two favorite sports: "We must have football. What would this country be without football in October?" and "The reason most people play golf is to wear clothes they would not be caught dead in otherwise." Apart from Payne Stewart and John Daly, I think that most golfers are safe from this distinction.

I was never really able to be an athlete. Growing up, I was epileptic, and excessive physical activity would cause seizures. As an adult, I didn't think that I had a chance in hell of accomplishing anything athletic.

I had a few friends at Centerpoint who liked to run half marathons, and they inspired me to want to train for one. I read a book by Jeff Galloway that proposed a different method called "Run, Walk, Run," meaning that you could run for a certain amount of time and then walk for a time to recover. Doing a marathon with this interval style seemed much more attainable to me, so I printed out one of his training schedules and put it on the refrigerator. It seemed pretty simple, so I started the next Monday morning, running/walking through Grand Terrace as the schedule suggested. I even found a great app that allows you to set up interval alarms for however long you run or walk. I started out with a small, ten-second run and one-minute brisk walking. Each day, I increased the run time by five to ten seconds and found that a thirty-second run and one-minute walk worked best for me. At about week three, my friend Stephanie was over, and she saw the running schedule on the fridge. She asked what it was about and then asked if I wanted a training partner. Did I ever, and she was the perfect taskmaster for me. She even said, "Now you're not going to call and cancel on me all the time, are you?"

Well, after a statement like that, you can rest assured that I never called to cancel, mainly out of spite! We trained for weeks, about twenty miles total per week, with our longest runs occurring on Saturdays, where we would increase the miles every week until we got to mile twelve, which meant that we were ready for a half marathon. Steph trained with me for eight weeks, and then things came up, and she could no longer train with me on Saturdays, so at the nine mile mark Evan took over with no training at all, saying only that his hips hurt a bit the following day. Men are amazing creations. He trained with me every Saturday from then on, and also ran the marathon with me. That first one was in San Diego, so we drove down the night before, and using a gift card given to us from Ashley's husband, Mike, we dined at Mister A's Steakhouse. We were informed that the special was a rib-eye steak with all the fixings, like salad, mashed potatoes, and broccolini. That sounded good to us, so we both ordered the special.

When we got the bill, Evan was noticeably distressed. It seems the special was sixty dollars each, so our bill with tip was around $180.00. Our gift card was generous at $90.00, but Evan had to pay the other half of the bill and was not happy about it. We very rarely order specials without asking for the price anymore.

Woke up feeling good and had my coffee and bagel with salmon and cream cheese breakfast. I was concerned because as you run, there is that impact, and your bowels tend to want to move, so I was hoping to go before we left because I don't like using portable potties, especially for that! Didn't happen, so I just hoped that I could get through the whole thirteen miles without need. There were a lot of people running this race, and we were toward the back of the pack, where all of the slow-moving people were. We began the run, and everything was going well when this little old lady, who had to have been in her eighties, came alongside us and said hello. We said hello back, and then she passed us. A little while later, we passed her, and so we went back and forth until the HILL, a very steep and punishing grade toward the end of the race. She passed us by, and we never saw her again.

So much for self-glorification when you're beaten by an old lady. Even so, I couldn't believe that I actually ran a half marathon and didn't die! We did another one some months later, which was a better fit: no-hills, very cool day, and a slight drizzle. I had decided to wear shorts for this race and unfortunately with the drizzle and my legs rubbing together, I started to blister. It was painful, and I had to wait for two miles before we would come upon a help station to get some salve. We finished, but it was grueling. It took a week for my legs to heal. Hard lesson to learn.

A few months after this, I found another race for us to train for, but at the six-mile point, I decided that I had had enough of 13.1 and would never run another race. They have plenty of races around here, so I may just have to train for a 10K run sometime in the future.

Culture

Our first venture into the arts as a couple was to see the musical Les Miserables at the Pantages Theater in Los Angeles. I love the parts of the book that I have read and the film versions and have listened to the score from the Broadway show MANY times. Evan secretly purchased tickets and surprised me with them for my Birthday. It was a first for Evan and a second for me, as I got to see The Phantom of the Opera musical with my co-workers at IBF. There were all types of people wearing all types of attire. Some were dressed formally, and others in blue jeans. We went with "dressy casual," having dinner at a nearby restaurant and then the show. It was a magical Birthday for me and was my 40th. Evan had turned 34 earlier in the year, so this was his time to be able to tell people that I was six years older than him – the things that give him satisfaction. We would go on to see a few more musicals, Cats, Anything Goes, and Peter Pan. Having been to New York three times now and have yet to hit opera season makes me a little sad, but should we ever plan another trip to the East Coast, I will insist on having a trip to The Met as part of the itinerary. How I would love to see Madame Butterfly or La Boheme at the Met.

We saw many shows at The Redlands Bowl as well as symphonies at The California Theater in San Bernardino and The Los Angeles Symphony on a few occasions. One of the best things about Evan is that he is willing to experience just about any form of art. We have yet to go to a ballet, but he is willing to.

He even stayed awake for a local production of "Proof" performed by The Driftwood Players of Aberdeen.

When I first met Evan, and for YEARS of our marriage, he listened exclusively to Christian music. I go through periods where I listen to something specific and only that one thing until it's time to move on to the next thing. I'm extremely picky, though, so I don't like the radio because it's forcing me to listen to things I don't like and how they repeat playlists so that you are constantly hearing the same songs. As aforementioned, I don't like much of any music after the 1970s, and I especially like listening to rock oldies while in the car, thereby forcing Evan to listen to my worldly music. Some artists Evan had never even heard of, but he gradually began to like my music, especially Crosby, Stills, Nash and Young, James Taylor, America, The Beatles, and The Rolling Stones. If I want to torture him, I'll listen to Barbra Streisand or Hank Williams. We just discovered Chris Stapleton and the Outlaw Country sound, so we are both listening to that frequently. Evan used to make fun of my old school country, but he has come to like it, especially Johnny Cash and Charlie Rich. Growing up with two parents who loved and collected a wide variety of music as well as older sisters who were kind enough to allow their pestering little sister to listen along with them to their favorites, gave me an appreciation for many music genres and I like just about anything other than metal, hip hop, rap, punk, and techno. Kim introduced me to The Beatles, Neil Young, and Dan Fogelberg. Barb liked The Stones and Jethro Tull, and Sherry liked The Righteous Brothers and The Mamas and the Papas. I have them all in my vinyl collection, and it is growing and pretty good, if I don't say so myself.

Our foray into painted art began with a documentary about the painter Bob Ross and his wet-on-wet technique that made him famous. During the intermission, an advertisement came on for a DVD set, with one of Ross' students teaching the same technique. We ordered the videos and then readied ourselves by purchasing some blank canvases, oil paints, brushes, thinner, and an air purifier because we wanted to paint in our bedroom, and Evan was afraid that the fumes would damage our brains. We painted as we watched the videos, and it was true, this wet-on-wet technique was really easy and with the instructions on highlighting and mixing colors, we were able to produce some not terrible landscape paintings. It was fun and just another thing for us to do together. As time went on, we got a bit too busy and didn't paint a great deal, but Evan is a natural, and he has always been able to use his artistic skills in his business as a painting and decorating contractor.

One of his clients invited us to dinner one night, and as we were visiting, he told the story about when he had asked Evan for a lead time to have his cabinets refinished, and it wasn't fast enough for him. He then hired a couple of ladies for the job and they had done the work that was before us. It looked terrible, and they didn't even bother to remove the doors or at least tape off the hinges so as not to get paint on them. I guess they even got paint on his dog, and after paying them $20,000 for the job, he wished that he had just waited for Evan. Well, this inspired Evan to increase his knowledge of faux finishing, so he enrolled in a certificate program at Faux Masters Studios in Yorba Linda, CA.

This was a learn-by-doing program, so when he was finished with the course, he walked away with many sample boards to show to potential clients, one of whom told him that he could frame these samples and sell them as abstract art. He told her that he hated abstract art, but her words got him thinking, and when his mind starts on an idea, there is no stopping him from pursuing it. This led to his decision to create an art piece for this client and present it to them as a wedding gift. Using colors existing in the design of their home, he created a beautiful 48x60 work of art called "It is Finished," the title being as much as their job finally being finished, their engagement culminating into a marriage, and the Holy Spirit led work itself depicting Jesus on the cross declaring "It is Finished." The painting was a hit and inspired Evan to continue creating artwork, and he would go on to show his work on both coasts and have his work displayed in other parts of the world.

In 2015, we owned an art gallery. I mentioned it before, but it's coming to fruition is a story in itself. My friend Cindy Walker told me about a cooperative gallery that was looking for artists to join. I was excited to meet with the director about my joining as a photographer. Because the director was a man, I couldn't meet with him alone, so Evan came to the meeting with me. I don't know what came over him, but he started talking about co-directing, and that he would help renovate a space, and since he had already renovated The Artist Eye Gallery, he was the best person to do it. A space was found in Downtown Redlands, perfect for a small gallery. It had been a nail salon, and it was a mess, but Evan spent a month working 16-hour days in order to be ready to open in September. We had over 500 people come by the gallery on Opening Night.

We set up the gallery much like The Artist Eye, and it was decided that the three directors, unnamed person, Evan, and myself, would man the gallery instead of trying to require and schedule other artists to do so. This meant that along with the ministry and getting my mom to and from her doctor's appointments, I had another thing on my plate in an already frazzled existence. I did all of the administrative work while the three of us curated. We were featured a couple of times in the local newspaper, and we had great success selling art. There weren't many days gone by where we wouldn't have at least one sale, but it was all taking a toll on me. I was doing Type A personality, turbo style; driving too fast, rushing from one appointment to another, staff meetings, classes to study for and teach, events for the ministry, and artist's receptions for the gallery. All of this was going on, and Evan was still showing in Laguna Beach and needing to be there at least three times per month. I still think back on all of this and thank God for getting me through it with a still sane mind and no speeding tickets or accidents on the freeway. I'm exhausted now after writing this and need to take a break.

We decided, after one year, to hand the gallery over to one of our resident artists as we were just stretched too thin, and our relationships with a few people had been damaged. The gallery is still open but is now a non-profit collaborative. I'm so happy that our work was not in vain and that many people were blessed by their experience, whether showing with us or purchasing artworks that we offered.

Gallery visiting has been one of our longstanding favorite things to do. Our gallery viewing is very different, though; Evan likes to scan and then revisit something that catches his eye quickly. I like to look at EVERYTHING and spend time with each piece, so he is almost always waiting for me either outside the gallery or getting into conversation with the gallery owner, allowing me the time to enjoy myself fully. There are usually several art galleries in whichever city we are visiting, so we are never without them. We have yet to do any of the Washington art museums, and there are quite a few to visit when we have the time. We have been to MANY art museums, from world-famous ones like the Metropolitan Museum of Art in New York to locally famous ones like The Norton Simon, Museum of Modern Art, The Getty, and The Broad. Like galleries, I want to see everything in the museum, so it does take us a long time to get through them. We are sometimes appalled by some of the things that are featured, being called art. For example, at MOMA, we turned a corner and there on a wall was a faucet; nothing else, just a faucet. Hmm.

If I could go anywhere in the world, I would go to Paris because she has everything: Art, Architecture, Food, captivating Views, Monet's Garden, and Opera. Not sure if I'll ever get there, but I know that Heaven and Eternity with Jesus will far surpass anything that this world has to offer so I'll be fine if I don't.

Part Four

Wrapping it Up

A Vision

June, 2019. Having fully recovered from our whirlwind vacation, I had returned to my morning routine of coffee with Evan, followed by pet feeding and finally time to read. I have always loved reading in the morning, whatever it may be: The Bible, spiritual growth, Christian living, classic literature. This particular day I was reading a book by Dick Eastman, "Intercessory Worship," and I "heard" The Lord say, "These live paintings and the preaching of the gospel, that you did on the road, will be a model for you in the future; to bring lost souls into My Kingdom. As you share with others My love and healing power, it will result in a great harvest!" Now, any time that I have a thought that I truly believe is from God, I write it down and tuck it away. As I couldn't look past the week, let alone think about the future it would have to be set aside, our mission to bring the power of knowing and following Jesus into troubled marriages took precedence over everything else.

A few months passed, and we got some news that would send me into another mourning period. Our church was going through some changes, and many people would have to cut back on their hours and expenses while they figured out what to do. We were part of the many. I began crying and couldn't stop for days. I tried to explain to Evan how I felt, and we even spoke to Pastor Dane about it. He assured me that our positions were secure, but I just knew that there was a major change coming and all would be lost. Eventually, I had to give my fears and concerns over to God since He holds our futures in His mighty and loving hand anyway.

In October, Evan decided that he would finally do some of the much-needed projects on the house and wanted to refinance and take out an equity line to pay for the work. I was a bit hesitant on the matter because I hate going further into debt for ANYTHING, but I eventually agreed to do it. About a month later, our friend Phil, who had moved to Washington a few years before, called Evan and asked him when he was going to come and visit him. Evan asked when he was going to have a job for him in Washington, so Phil sent him blueprints for a job to bid in Bellevue, WA, one of the most expensive areas in the United States.

Evan spent about a week on the bid, and after he sent it, he decided that he had better think about what we would do if he were to get the job. Would we all go to Washington or just him? What would we do about our jobs? Was there a less expensive area where we could stay, and he could commute from? So Evan is looking online and on the Airbnb app while I'm thinking to myself, "Now that Mom is gone, there isn't any reason why we couldn't move to the Pacific Northwest and start a new life." So I'm looking on the Redfin and Trulia Apps to find affordable houses for us to purchase. I really wanted to be able to sell our home and have a huge down payment or be able to pay outright for a home. Astoria's prices had risen considerably, so I started to look at nearby places like Seaside and Warrenton. I found the PERFECT house in Warrenton as it had a large lot for all of Evan's stuff, and the house was awesome, AND at $250,000, it was affordable.

We didn't hear from Phil about the job thing, and we got busy doing other stuff, so that calmed down a little, but I was still thinking about it.

December, 2019. We signed our loan papers on Friday, the sixth. We would have a considerable amount of cash in our bank account in just a few days' time. Our couples ministry was flourishing, and several groups were planning Christmas parties. We had plans to attend two of them the next day. The first party was in the afternoon. I was enjoying seeing everyone, and I noticed that Evan was standing alone, just watching everyone, with a sort of pleased look on his face. God had done great things in this ministry, and here we were, enjoying some of the fruits of our labor.

We said our goodbyes and headed to the next party, a more formal one. After dinner and an ornament exchange, I was tired from an already packed couple of days, so we got up to go home, and while we were saying our goodbyes, a man that we barely knew looked up at us and said, "OK guys, look around at the faces you won't see next Christmas!" Perplexed, we made our way to the car, and Evan asked if I had heard what Doug said. I said, "Yeah, look at the faces you won't see next Christmas. What do you think that means?" He didn't have a clue, so we drove home in silence, considering its meaning. I was not looking forward to working the next day because I knew that I would be tired in the morning from being out so late.

Sunday, December 8th. Coffee, breakfast, phones out; Evan looking on maps for possible places to stay if the Washington job happened and me, looking on Trulia for other possible houses to move into while he was working up north. He suddenly asked if I had ever heard of Aberdeen, Washington. I said that I hadn't, and so he googled Aberdeen, WA, and this picture popped up of a man under a bridge, shooting heroin into his arm. He showed it to me, and we were both shocked and saddened that such a picture was representative of an entire area.

We got to Centerpoint to attend the 9:15 service and then teach a marriage class at 10:45. The worship began and during the song, "Way Maker," as we sang the chorus, "way maker, miracle worker, promise keeper, light in the darkness", I was taken out of my seat and placed in front of a very large screen. A movie was playing, a very old silent black and white with flickering and grainy film. There was complete and utter darkness everywhere, all except this Little A-Frame House in the middle of the screen. It had large windows, and as I got closer to see inside, I saw Evan and myself, and we were worshipping and interceding for Aberdeen. I burst into tears, telling God that I didn't want to go to Aberdeen, WA, to start a church!

Back in my seat, people still singing, Evan asked me what was the matter. I told him that I couldn't talk about it right then, plus we had a class to teach. It would just have to wait until later. After class, we skipped going to lunch with the regular group and got takeout for home. I told Evan about the vision and asked if we could change our vacation plan, road-tripping to Aberdeen instead of going to South Carlsbad for camping, to see if God was really calling us to go there. He agreed and so on December 18th, we left Grand Terrace and got to Seaside Oregon as quickly as possible, staying one night in an old Bed and Breakfast that literally moved with the intense seaside wind. Crazy but really cool place, The Gilbert Inn. The next day, we stopped at Cape Disappointment (it was closed) and just sat in the parking area for a while, listening to the wind howling and the crashing waves of the angry sea. We found a nice hotel in Ocean Shores, The Canterbury Inn, which has ocean views and beautifully kept condos. We planned to relax for the next two days to celebrate my birthday, so Evan went out and got us food several times, and we went out for dinner on the second night. We checked out and explored the city of Ocean Shores. Not many restaurants, small grocery stores, and many undeveloped properties, it didn't seem like a place that we would want to live coming from Southern California with fast food on every corner and literally thousands of businesses from which to choose for your every need or desire. That thought went out the window as my eyes looked upon the house from my vision, an A- frame home with large windows on the front. I gasped and told Evan to back up because there it was, and it was for sale!! We found the listing agent and asked to see it. She said that the owners lived in Seattle, and the house was actually leased to a couple, and one of them had just had a major surgery, so she wasn't sure if it would be possible to see it. She would get back to us in a few days, so we left Ocean Shores for Aberdeen to see what God would say.

December 22, Sunday. We looked online for nearby churches, and we decided to attend the River of Life. A smaller congregation was just what we needed on this particular day, and we really enjoyed it. We met Pastor Doug and his wife, Nancy, and they invited us to go to lunch with them and a few other people. We told them our story, and they told us about Grays Harbor and its logging history. After lunch, we went exploring. There is an area in Aberdeen that has beautiful homes on a grand hilltop. We found an empty property and wondered if a home could be built there. Evan distinctly remembered that God spoke to him, saying, "I don't want you to live above them; I want you to live among them." We took this as another sign from Him that we would live in this area sometime in the future. For the next few days, we rested in the mornings and went exploring in the afternoons. Westport, Montesano, Forks, Back to Ocean Shores to drive out onto the beach and just sit in the car listening to the waves. Of course, no one else was out there. It was cold and very windy. In Southern California, there are people on the beach in every season and in every type of weather, so it was a little eerie being out there by ourselves. We received a call from the real estate agent about the house in Ocean Shores. They could allow us to see the house, but not until Friday, and we had planned to leave that day, so we went back to the Canterbury Inn for an additional night and would see the house the next morning. Our room was incredible, especially because there was a giant bathtub in the only bedroom of the condo. I laughed and told Evan that I didn't know what he was going to be doing later, but I would be in that giant tub relaxing for several hours! Of course, he joined me, and this would start a new trend in our marriage: bathtub time. We don't even have a giant bathtub right now, but since we both fit and it is a great way to have face-to-face communication time, we still engage in the activity. TMI?

We packed up our things and headed over to the house on Octopus Ave. When we got into the house, we both immediately said, NO WAY! There was mold on the ceilings, and the kitchen was barely functional. It also had a very strange odor, so we couldn't wait to get out of there. We went back to the real estate office and asked about all of the undeveloped properties that were for sale around town. They printed out a list for us, with photos, and as soon as we got the list, I saw a BEAUTIFUL property that had already been cleared and had water, sewer, and power already finished and ready to go. What caught my eye in the photo was the way that the sunset shone through a group of trees at the very back of the property. It was so majestic; I was excited to get there. We found out that the lot next to this one was also included in the price, but it hadn't been excavated yet, and it was filled with beautiful evergreen trees! Ever since we took our first trip to Northern California, we had both wanted to find a place that had ocean views as well as tall evergreens like the redwood trees. This was almost perfect and probably as close as we would get to that dream, so we made inquiries about financing empty lots and made a decision to race home and possibly purchase the property on Snahapish Avenue in Ocean Shores. After all, it DID face the direction of Aberdeen, and it was only a thirty-minute drive to Aberdeen.

December 28th, Saturday. We arrived in the late afternoon to find the house, and everyone in it doing well. Pepper was hyperventilating, so happy to see us, and Tucker was a bit standoffish for a while, but he finally came around. Charlie could not have cared less about our arrival, and he just wanted to go outside. We had dinner with Janice at Baker's, oh, how I miss Baker's, and she went back to her place, and we relaxed, happy to be home.

January 6th, Monday. Evan got home from work and was still on a call that he had taken on his way. He was talking to a loan agent from Timberland Bank about the Snahapish property. I waited patiently for him, and while we had dinner, he told me the story. He had spoken to Dan, the bank VP, about our wanting to purchase the land now and then build our dream home in the near future. Dan said that we could purchase the property, but we wouldn't be able to get a loan for the building until Evan had been in business in Washington for at least two years.

He said that he could find out what we pre-qualified for, and then we should purchase a house now, then sell it and build a home later. He called back the next day with a number, $140,000. It would have been more, but since we still had a mortgage on the California house, this would be enough to at least start the process. Now, we could begin the search for a house in Aberdeen, not Ocean Shores, as everything there was out of our price range. Most of our spare time for the next few weeks would be spent looking for properties and wondering what God would have us do. I found a house that was A-framed and had an enclosed sunporch with large windows looking out to the neighborhood, but then I looked at the interior photos and got sad because it had been a rental for many years, and Evan would not enjoy undoing many years of bad touch-ups and poorly done work. Even though I knew that he wouldn't want this one, I still put it in my favorites folder just in case. It was also the right price, $140,000.

Evan called me during lunch and said that he found a house that had a property attached to it. It had been asphalted and used for extra parking for a business located behind the two properties.

What if the owner would include the asphalt property as part of the selling price? That would definitely be a sign from God as this would solve all of Evan's problems with having a place to store all of his trailers and work equipment. He asked if I had seen the little A-framed house with the sunporch. WHAT??!! That's my house, the one that I want! I messaged Nancy from River of Life and asked if she knew a real estate agent who had integrity and could help us long-distance. She gave me a name, Joy, my Momma's name, and I liked that. She was wonderful and sent the offer to the owner's agent, and he accepted our offer! We were stunned. We had only been away from Aberdeen for a few weeks, and having only spent a short amount of time there, we were buying a house.

Some people thought we were nuts. We hadn't even seen the property; how could we buy it? Well, we did finally see it for the inspection. We flew into SeaTac airport, rented a car, and headed out to Aberdeen. The house was actually located in the neighboring city of Hoquiam, a place that we only quickly drove through when on our way in or out of Aberdeen when we first visited. When we walked in, we both noticed the sloping floor, obviously a foundation issue, but to what extent, we wouldn't find out until a year later. The paint was awful, but everything else was ok by me. Evan wasn't impressed, but it would meet all of our needs, and he could fix just about anything, so he was game, too. The inspection showed very old knob and tube electrical wiring, and he could see some foundation trouble, so it would have to be looked at by a professional. It was looked at, and we made a counter-offer due to the cost of the repairs needed.

The seller agreed AND paid our closing costs as well. We went back to California and waited for loan docs to be sent, and on February 29th, 2020, Evan drove to Aberdeen, Washington, picked up the keys to our home, painted the ugly gray walls of the living and dining rooms a beautiful soothing blue, did a few other projects and drove home, stopping at Ashley's on the way. It was now time to tell everyone that we would be moving away, leaving our positions, leaving Evan's business clients. It was hard. There were a lot of tears. There was a lot of packing to do, and I just didn't know how I would do all of it as Evan was working seven days a week and for long hours, trying to get all of his promised jobs completed.

I had never packed a whole household. I always just had my minuscule belongings before, but now there was TONS of stuff to go through, get rid of, and decide if we would have room for. The new place had almost no storage, the three closets were small, and we both had much clothing. I can't even imagine having that much now, but we had a great deal of storage and closet space for all of our stuff in that house. I felt paralyzed and couldn't face the huge task. A few months went by, and I still had done very little. I asked a few friends if they would be willing to come over and help me. Seven of the most wonderful people in the world came over on a Saturday, worked for over eight hours, and packed up almost the entire house. Kat, Lissa, Kelly, Tim and Christie, Coleen, and Mary thank you for rescuing me!

When it was time to get everyone lunch at Miguel's, another place that I miss terribly, one of the helpers asked how much his lunch was going to cost. Like, I'm going to let any of them pay for their lunch! I would probably still be in California, with a house full of stuff to pack, had these friends not been there to help.

We returned to Hoquiam three times to do projects. It was easy to do this because Covid 19 caused the shutdown of large gatherings, so we now did classes and watched church services online. We got our internet installed and did our classes right here. It wasn't great for Evan when he needed to go to Home Depot. They could only allow so many people into the store at once, so he would have to wait in line for an hour sometimes. He knocked down a wall and chimney, built a new wall, and got rid of the biggest eyesore in our neighborhood, replacing it with a landscaped and fenced rock garden that everyone in the neighborhood commented on. He built a fence around our whole property, did more painting, put up curtains, finished up the guest room so that we would have a nice place to relax, put in a new water line on the asphalt side, and so much more.

The last thing that we did before driving back to Cali for the last time was to clean the floors so that we could move the furniture right in when we moved me up here for good.

September 6th, Sunday. After zooming with our Marriage Group, we headed to Anaheim to look at a truck to purchase. As the Hoquiam house had no garage, we were perplexed about what we were going to do with all of his tools and other supplies for his business. We found a storage trailer that he thought would be big enough, if he were to take only what he needed and not all of the stuff that he had accumulated over the years for possible future projects. The trailer would be too heavy to pull with his Ram 1500 truck, so we were going to purchase a new Ram 2500 with a Cummins diesel engine. Man, are those things expensive, not to mention that we would need to finance it. We already had two mortgages, and now this sixty-thousand-dollar machine would be added to it. Would we even be able to get a loan on it? I am still surprised that we were able to drive away with that truck that very afternoon, and we would go to the trailer place the next day to see if we could finance that as well. So another fourteen thousand was added to the total of our heavily financed venture, roughly about five hundred thousand. Hard to believe.

I think it goes back to the belief that this was God's will for us, and so He would make sure that we came out of this in good shape.

October 3rd, 2020. Trailer loaded, Check. (more amazing friends came over to help us load) Animals in my car, Check. Airpods in and music from phone playing, Check. We got on the road mid-morning, as usual, and would be stopping for two nights on the way to Hoquiam. Tucker and Pepper both slept on the floor of the passenger side until later in the day when Tucker decided that he would be more comfortable on my lap. He was so thin by now, and I wasn't sure how long he would be with us, so I put up with having a hot cat on my lap while driving. When we arrived at our home, Phil and Karen were there to help Evan unload the trailer as I directed traffic. There was so much that still needed going through as this house was considerably smaller than the Grand Terrace one. We still have a whole room packed with boxes to go through, and I've lived here for almost three years!

I was home, and I loved it. I loved the weather, the rain and cloudy cool days. I would sit on my sun porch for hours, reading and sometimes napping. Pepper liked it, too. She could see everyone walking by and loved barking at them. She also got used to going potty in the rain and now loves taking walks around the neighborhood. One particular morning, I realized something; in my vision, there was a sign that said Aberdeen on it, so we always assumed that it just stood for the whole area where we lived now, but I noticed for the first time and put it all together, that the sign was a street sign: Aberdeen Ave., Our street, the street where we now live! Only God can make such a thing happen. Only He could have convinced me that this was the place for us to live. Had He given Evan the vision, I would have told him that God needed to give me the vision, too. We would probably still be living in California or maybe somewhere else, but not in a little town without even a Chipotle or Chick-fil-A. It is just as well; when we have a vast array of amazing food choices, we would frequent, and we did frequent them far too often. Here, we have two McDonald's, two Dairy Queens, Arby's, Jack in the Box, Wendy's, Taco Bell, Burger King, four pizza places to choose from, a fine dining restaurant, a good Sushi place, and countless taverns with food. We go to Olympia at least once a month to go to Costco and a larger Home Depot store.

It's only an hour's drive, and it's a pretty one with lots of tall trees and very little traffic. There, all of our favorite food places exist, but we have had more fun trying to find other places to eat besides the well-known ones. I could really go for some Chipotle tacos right now, though, but I'm at home, so I will have to make tacos myself.

The speed limit here in town is 30mph, a dismal thing for me unless I'm driving my old Dodge D-100 truck, Annie; she only likes going slow anyway. We picked up Annie on one of our trips to work on the house. I told Evan that I wanted an old truck to drive around in, so I started looking on Craigslist for one near Hoquiam. I found the perfect one in Chehalis, about an hour from the house, so I arranged for the owner to meet us, and we both drove the truck. Everything was fine, except Evan didn't like the price, so they negotiated while I sat in the truck, ready to drive it it's new home in Hoquiam. We had to stop for gas, and as I parked at the pump, Evan noticed water leaking from the engine compartment. We looked at the radiator, and there was a hole that the water was coming out of. We called AAA and towed the truck to Hoquiam. We decided to call her Annie, after Mom, and even though we have put money into making her drive better, she's still old and cranky when it's cold outside. On warm days, she starts right up and drives fine. It is cold here much more often than warm, so she is mostly a summer driver.

Evan had to return to California to finish his jobs and get the house ready to put on the market. It would be seven months before he would be here full-time. We survived by Zooming every night, most times from our respective bathtubs, as well as Evan flying up here for a week every few months. When the house was ready, our agent and longtime friend, Karen Aaker, received a call from a family looking to move to Grand Terrace from Long Beach. They offered us five thousand over asking, and so before the house was even formally listed, it was sold.

The best part was that our equity in the house was enough to pay for our new house in full, and a gift from Karen allowed us to pay for the trailer in full as well. Now, we only had one loan for the truck. God did that and so much more. Evan told me that when it was time for him to leave California, God would turn the light switch off in California and turn it on in Washington for his business. He wasn't wrong.

Mom

July 18, 2023. Today is Mom's Birthday. She would have been 85. Mom was my "person in this world," meaning that she understood and knew me better than anyone else. When I was happy about something, she was the first person that I wanted to tell about it. If I was down, she always knew it. If I needed help, she was there with me, and if she couldn't help, she encouraged me to get the help that I needed. She also gifted me with her stubborn spirit, love for sweets and Sinatra, vanity, and the ability to show love to people in a tangible way. She had her own fan club no matter where she tended bar. She had the most beautiful green eyes that were so full of life. She was loved by so many, but especially by her children.

She wasn't perfect, but to me, she was the best person on earth. Now Evan has the spot, and he isn't even jealous that he was second to Mom. He was there with me when Mom's health took a turn, and he never complained if I had to be with her in a time of crisis, leaving him to fend for himself.

In 2013, Mom was diagnosed with lung cancer in both lungs, but she didn't have one cancer. She had two separate cancers, a miracle. This meant that her cancer hadn't spread, and it was caught soon enough to hopefully contain it.

Chemotherapy wasn't effective for her type of cancer, so she was sent to a Palm Desert radiology office where they had a stereotactic radiation machine. This form of radiation is different in that the tumor receives a very high level of radiation while the surrounding tissue receives a much lower dose, minimizing side effects.

She would need only five treatments on each lung, taking about six weeks to complete. I drove her to her appointments in my Mini Cooper, which she loved, and we would spend time talking and listening to Il Volo, with Mom napping on occasion. I was proud of the fact that she would sleep in a car that I was driving. These radiation treatments would still take a heavy toll on her physically. The amount of radiation was large, and even though it was concentrated in one precise area, there would still be damage to her overall health. Many of her health issues from before the treatments were now accelerated, so she had to have several major surgeries to alleviate pain from stenosis as well as suffering with arthritic issues, causing her to be in pain a great deal of the time. She didn't let any of this keep her from enjoying her life; she knew that she was given a gift from God, having been given more time. We didn't know how much time she would have, but I spent every moment that I could with her. I would spend a great deal of time taking her to doctor's appointments in the five years that she survived cancer. In 2016, I stopped by her house one time since I had to go to a store just up the street from her, and Art was cleaning her foot. As soon as I saw it, I freaked out. She had a huge crater on the bottom of her foot, and you could tell it was infected. She never even felt it. We wrapped it up and took her to my car and over to her primary physician's office. As soon as the doctor saw me, she asked where Mom was and had me bring her into an examining room. No appointment, no check-in.

She examined her foot and phoned an associate who was a wound specialist. We had an appointment for the next day, and it took months for her foot to heal. Of course, I was spending time and not minding taking her at all; even though I FELT like my life was out of control, I had to remain in control so that I could help her through whatever health crisis she was dealing with. It took almost a year for the wound to heal, but it would come back as pressure ulcers often do. In 2018, we rushed her to the ER as the wound was grossly infected. She was admitted and the next evening she went into septic shock. They had to use a defibrillator to regulate her heart after she went in Afib. I stood in the hall and watched with the eerie feeling of having seen this before. Of course, I had, every week for so many years while watching ER on television. This was the real thing and scary. She was intubated and taken to the ICU, and Tiff and I had to wait for hours for a doctor to speak to us. Evan came too and would go to the cafeteria any time we needed anything. In total, Mom was in ICU for ten days. She didn't wake up for seven of those days, and when she did, they had trouble weaning her off the oxygen, so she had to remain intubated while they did some tests. Her pulmonologist informed us that she had a lot of fluid that had built up around her lungs, and he wanted to do a last-ditch procedure to drain the fluid and relieve the pressure in her lungs. Art and I agreed that it was worth the risk, so her lungs were drained of two liters of fluid, and they were able to extubate her and transfer her to a telemetry unit for seven days. Because of the infection, she had to remain on IV antibiotics, and so we had to send her to a skilled nursing facility, probably the most difficult thing I ever had to do because I knew that she would be miserable and I wouldn't be allowed to stay with her. I had stayed at the hospital day and night, except to go home to shower so that she wouldn't be so upset.

She had plenty of people who wanted to visit, but Mom didn't really like having visitors when she was hospitalized for any reason, but she did allow a few people to come. She would remain there for another 23 days, and even though it was really tough, I was so proud of her for being a great patient (she always was) and doing all of her physical therapy so that she could go home stronger.

Mom continued to improve and even went back to singing karaoke at Post 106. She also continued to have her Wacky

Wednesdays with her lady friends. They celebrated her 80th Birthday with a big party for her and several other ladies who would be turning 80 that year. They even made-up special shirts for all of them. It was always wonderful to know that Mom was loved so much by everyone who knew her.

We saw her pulmonologist in early October, and he told us that with the information he had at the time, she could have a year or so left. Eventually, her lungs would give out from all of the trauma. She took it pretty well and decided just to make the most of each day that she had. A few weeks later, Tiff and I took her to see the new A Star is Born movie (we all loved it), and Mom fell asleep a couple of times. We woke her up, though, and she saw it again with Aunt Susie a few weeks after that. Her foot was getting worse again, so we saw her vascular specialist, and he said that she was healthy enough to have an angiogram to help open up her circulation. The procedure went really well, but she had some blood pressure issues afterward, so she was in the ICU for a couple of days and then returned home a few days later. Her primary ordered a PET scan for her, so we got that scheduled.

Tiff and her fiancé had decided to get married sooner rather than later so that Mom could be there, so we went wedding dress shopping with Tiff, and then I took Mom for her PET scan at the hospital. She was getting tired more easily, but she seemed alright. The next week, she was not feeling very well. She thought that she had a cold but went to Wacky Wednesday anyway. When she got home, she told Art to call an ambulance, she was having a lot of trouble breathing. I got to the hospital as quickly as I could, and Tiff was already there. Mom was on a forced air machine, kind of like a CPAP on steroids, when the ER doctor came in. He told her that she would need to get her affairs in order because she only had a few days to live.

She had not yet signed a DNR (Do Not Resuscitate) order, and that was part of what he meant. She looked at him and said, "That's not possible, I have plans!" but he assured her that he was correct in his assessment and even had Tif and I go to see the results of her PET scan from last week. I asked, "Where is her lung?" He said, "Precisely, it is gone, and the other one has a large mass in it. She will have to stay or be discharged on Hospice." I asked her what she wanted to do, and since she had already spoken to a lovely hospice representative, a few weeks before, she opted to go home. It was Thanksgiving Eve, and we didn't know if we could get someone to arrange everything, but this amazing lady drove 30 miles in traffic to make all of the arrangements and saw us through to the very end. It was a great privilege for Evan and I to be able to take care of Mom when we got her home. Hospice provided everything that we needed to keep her comfortable: medication, oxygen machines, 24-hour on-call nursing, etc.

On Thanksgiving morning, Mom asked me when I was going home to make the turkey and stuffing for dinner. I had not even thought about it, but Thanksgiving was her favorite holiday, so I went home, put the turkey in the oven, and stayed at home watching football until it was ready to transfer over to Mom and Art's. This would be her last meal, and Tiff and I both were happy that we were there to cook and eat her last meal with her. She would be lucid for several more days, really only being unconscious her last two days. The night before she passed away, we had an enormously stressful situation; I was sitting on the couch reading while Evan and Mom slept. Suddenly, the electricity shut off, and we were in the dark! Mom's machines stopped running, and I panicked, woke up Evan; and he ran out to the electrical box to find the breaker and turn it back on. It worked for about twenty seconds and shut off again. I'm on the phone by now because we were pretty sure that one of the oxygen machines was shorting out, tripping the breaker. We unplugged it so that the other one could continue to work and Mom never even missed a beat since she had on one of those masks that have a reserve. Art never even knew that anything had happened, so we tried our best to calm down while we waited for a new machine from Hospice. This was late at night, and they still came to our aid quickly. Once we had her hooked back up to a sufficient oxygen level, we were able to relax. Things were quiet the next day, and I remember wondering how long she could keep hanging on. After Tiff went home, I decided to take a nap, it was late, and Evan had rested earlier. He was sitting at the dining room table watching television on his phone, and I heard him laughing. I looked up to see what he was laughing about. He had just seen the newest Duluth Trading underwear commercial, and he couldn't stop laughing.

I got up to check on Mom, and she was barely breathing, only tiny short breaths. I called Tiff and told her that I was really sure, this time, that she was very close. I sat down beside her, and I took her hand. I told her, "When you see Jesus, just let go of my hand and take His" and she did. I felt many emotions-loss, joy, expectation, sorrow for my sisters who couldn't be there with her.

I miss her every day but Mother's Day and her birthday are the days when I miss her most. Tonight, Evan and I plan to celebrate her day by opening a bottle of champagne, given to us for our anniversary, toasting Mom and wishing she was here to toast the occasion with us. Mom didn't like champagne, but she would have joined us just the same.

These Days

When we fell in love with the Pacific Northwest, we had no idea where we would land, given that we like ALL of the PNW. Living in Hoquiam gives us the same kind of central location that we had in Grand Terrace when we lived there. We are about twenty miles from the beach, close to a slew of rivers to enjoy, have many camping situations to choose from, about two hours away from a major cultural center, and an hour away from any type of food we are craving at any given time. We have a major grocery but only one store, so it gets really crowded. We have several decent department stores and several dollar places. We're even major enough to have a very well-stocked and run Goodwill store as well as a Habitat for Humanity.

We found a church to attend that is a great place to bring any one of our neighbors who may decide to join us sometime in the future. Our home needs work, work that may or may not get done, but it is livable, and I love it. I have a garden, my second, and I love working in it, but I can't be in the sun too much, and my hands don't work very well, so our gardener has more duties than just mowing the lawn now. Evan's business is thriving, just like he said that it would. God is so faithful. We have everything that we need, including friends and neighbors who make life more enjoyable and complete.

Football will be here soon, and I'll be plenty occupied and happy for the next five months. Life is good.

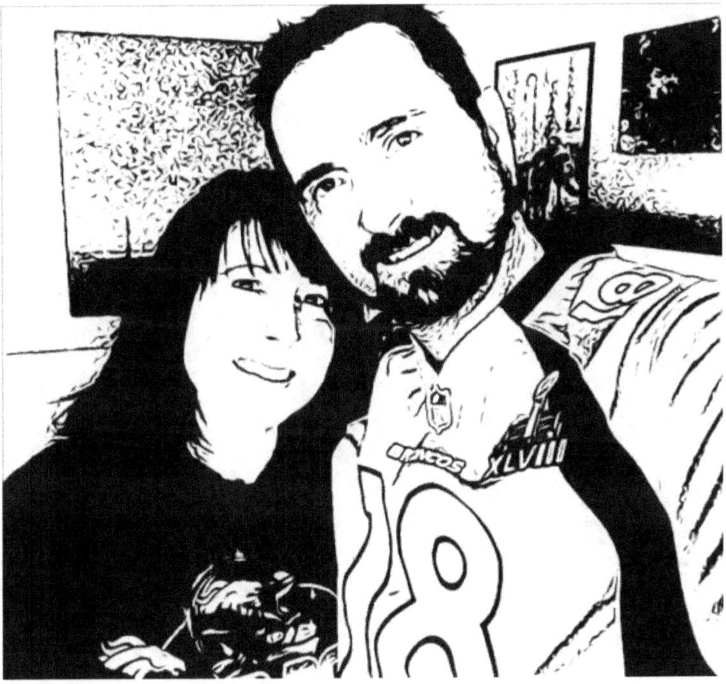
BRONCOS
XLVIII